D0710069

THE ETHIOPIAN TATTOO SHOP

had faded, blue window frames that wearily held its grey, dust-covered glass. I had attempted on my two previous visits to peer through the windows in order to see something of the inside of the tattoo shop. But like old-fashioned confessional screens they concealed well the secrets that were kept on the other side.

The sun was slowly descending behind the flat roof tops and the western walls of the Old City of Jerusalem on that early autumn afternoon in 1971. The narrow, stone-paved street was closely bordered by tall walls that

Written And Illuminated By Edward Hays

opened only onto occasional dark door-
ways of small shops or living quarters;
lingering in them were the aromas of
countless centuries.

The Old City of Jerusalem has the
magic ability to pinch the slim waist of
the hourglass of history and cause time
to stand still. I am sure that it was this
sense of enchantment — and the accom-
panying feeling of timelessness — that
had taken me by the hand and was now
leading me, once again, to the door of
the Ethiopian Tattoo Shop.

I stood with my right hand grasping
the door handle, and as I held it I felt
the fingerprints of thousands of Ethio-
pian-Coptic Christian pilgrims who had
touched it, turned it and entered to be
tattooed.

I was neither an Ethiopian nor a
*Coptic Christian, but I **was** a pilgrim to*
Jerusalem, the Holy City. A new friend
whom I had met while staying in the
Old City, Fr. Murray Rogers, a priest
and cosmic pilgrim who had recently
arrived from a long stay in India, had
introduced me to the small Ethiopian-
Coptic community which lived in the
Holy City.

They lived and worshipped on the

THE ETHIOPIAN TATTOO SHOP

copyright © 1983, by Edward M. Hays

Library of Congress Catalog Card Number: 83-82276
ISBN 0-939516-06-3

published by
Forest of Peace Books, Inc.
Route One – Box 247
Easton, Kansas 66020

printed by
Hall Directory, Inc.
Topeka, Kansas 66608

January 1984

roof of the Church of the Holy Sepulcher in that timeless ritual which echoed the life of Egyptian Christians of the earliest centuries. It was on my first visit to that sacred spot that I noticed their tattoos. The arms and hands of monks and nuns, and even of the bishop, had religious symbols tattooed on them. Somehow in ageless Jerusalem it all seemed logical. If you believed, really believed, then why not be branded with a sign of that belief?

Slowly, I did something that I had been unable to do on my first two visits: I opened the door to the tattoo shop. A small brass bell on the door jingled as my eyes refocused to the blue twilight-darkness of the tiny shop. On the wall directly in front of me, in a hand-carved, ornate wooden frame, was a picture of the Ethiopian Emperor, Haile Selassie. Behind the picture frame, draping to the right, was a faded and dusty green, yellow and red flag of Ethiopia.

It was upon ascending to the throne in 1928 that the Emperor chose the name Haile Selassie which means "Power of the Trinity." Looking into the face of that famous man, the "Lion of Judah, Elect of God, King of Kings of Ethiopia," I wondered if indeed it was the power of the Trinity that had brought me here to this shop, or was it the power of romanticism? I knew that I was a romantic, but I had always believed that I was, like John Kennedy, a realistic

7

romantic! My presence in a tattoo shop now challenged that belief. The tattoo of a Coptic cross on one's hand, an indelible drawing of the Theotokos, the Mother of God, on one's arm, or of some Byzantine cross on one's chest might be common in Jerusalem, or in Addis Ababa in Ethiopia, but what about in Kansas City?

To the left of the picture of Haile Selassie was a doorway. Across it, covering the opening, hung a dark, heavy drape. The doorway led, I supposed, to the owner's living quarters in the back of the shop. My eyes, now accustomed to the twilight, could see that the shop had a very low ceiling with aged, yellowing plaster walls. On the walls were illustrations of the hundreds of available designs. In the center of the small room was a wooden table and two wooden, straight-back chairs. On the table was a variety of stencil-like instruments, several tiny bottles and containers, a pile of soiled rags and a couple of empty coffee cups. Over the table, hanging from a single cord, was a light with a tin, funnel-like shade.

My right hand reached back for the door handle. My eyes were filled with the room and its contents, but my mind was filled with only one thought: escape to the street, retreat from the magic timelessness of the Old City. I was a pilgrim, one who journeys to holy places. But a pilgrim is also one who goes home after the pilgrimage. If I was tattooed, would that permanent, bodily brand of belief freeze me at one point in my journey of faith? Logic, or fear, or even common sense took charge, and I turned to leave. But just then the heavy drape over the doorway to the back room slowly began to move.

My hand released the door handle as my heart sank. From behind the curtain stepped a black man who appeared to be somewhere in his early sixties. He looked much like the other Ethiopians that I had seen

8

on the streets and on the roof of the Church of the Holy Sepulcher.

"You have come for a tattoo?" he asked as he moved from the dark shadows into the faded, yellow twilight of the late afternoon.

"I was only curious," I replied. "I thought I would merely stop in to inquire about the cost . . . I was . . . I thought . . . " My words trailed off as I searched for what to say. The eyes of the Ethiopian were of particular interest, especially his left eye which seemed to be watching a part of myself that even I had not yet seen.

"Are you a pilgrim or merely a tourist?" he asked as he came closer.

"I am a pilgrim," I answered. I knew how easy it is to also be a tourist, to **compromise** the pilgrimage with the adventures of a trip. To seek the holy in shrines and holy places calls for a unique style of traveling. A monk at the French monastery of Taize had asked me the same question but in another way. I thought I had made the decision to separate the pilgrimage from the trip. In deciding where to go, what to see and where to stay, I had made the choices simple. I was seeking only the holy but had come to realize, now halfway around the world, that its dwelling was everywhere!

"Do you want a tattoo?" He smiled as he spoke. His lips parted slightly and his eyes danced. His question swirled around the tiny room in a wild, taunting dance. That question surfaced memories of my childhood: the fear of the unknown, of pain, of the chill of the waters in the swimming pond; the fear of being caught or having to be a "real" man. They all joined hands in the ring-dance with his question and circled me in a blinding whirl.

"I have many designs, ancient, sacred and magical," he continued without a trace of a smile. "The

9

tattoo, you know, is more than some decoration. It holds the power to heal, to protect, to drive away evil spirits. It is your **passport**; you are a pilgrim, are you not?"

"Does it hurt?" I asked, surprising myself at the honesty of the question that seemed to come from somewhere deep, deep in the bottom of my being.

His right hand slowly reached out, and he placed it on my shoulder. The touch of his large hand calmed my heart which was racing wildly out of control, sounding retreat — escape to the narrow street that led to safety. His hand on my shoulder was an anchor holding me back from setting sail as he spoke, "No, you will feel nothing! For three generations my family has been tattooing our people who come to Jerusalem on pilgrimage. Not only are the designs ancient, so are the methods. I will tattoo you as my father, my grandfather and my great-grandfather tattooed — without pain!"

"But," I asked, "how is it that I will feel no pain? Do I take some drug?"

"No drug is used," he replied, "the method is most ancient. I will tell you a story, and it will so absorb you that there will be no room left in you for pain. My stories will shield you from all that hurts and will heal you of all that lies hidden within. I promise you; I know."

For the first time I noticed them. On his hands and arms were tattoos, and I could imagine that elsewhere on his body he was also inscribed with these mystical markings.

"Thank you," I replied. "I am sure that you are correct. But I am not sure — I mean, about getting a tattoo. I am an American, and in my home country tattoos are usually worn only by sailors and soldiers or by circus folk. I'm . . . I'm not sure."

"There will be no pain," he said, his hand lifting

10

from my shoulder and pointing to one of the chairs by the table. "Here, be seated; be my guest, please. Allow me to show you the magic power of a story. Please take a seat and simply close your eyes and listen. Each story is not long, but you will see how it can fill every corner of your consciousness."

My apprehension stopped tugging at my shirt sleeve and hesitated for a moment in its demands to escape. In that moment of time I found myself sitting down at the old wooden table in the center of the tattoo shop. Outside the dusty windows, the sun had disappeared in the west, burying itself somewhere beyond the walls of the Old City. Darkness, the invisible army of night, slid slowly over those walls and poured into the narrow, alley-like streets.

As the Ethiopian tattooist sat down, he reached up and turned on the single light that wore the funneled shade. A swaying circle of white light floated around the table, making me feel as if I were at sea. He was seated directly across from me, and that unique left eye welcomed me, caressing me, as if I were a friend unseen for years. As the slowly swaying circle of light washed over me, I knew that some great adventure was about to begin. He nodded at me as if he knew my thoughts, and then he began . . . .

LET THE EVIL SPIRITS, SPELLS
And ENCHANTERS BE CUT
BY THE SWORD of MICHAEL
And
PIERCED BY THE
LANCE
of
George

The Magi

Once upon a time, long ago, everything was perfect, and business had never been better. Temples and shrines were crowded with devotees, and monasteries were so full that they had to turn away applicants. The world was at peace, and each day life was getting better and better.

One night when the weather was mild and a warm breeze was blowing off the sea, many were sleeping on the rooftops of their homes. Even the stars seemed to have fallen asleep — slumbering with their lights left on. Suddenly in the distant western sky there appeared a bright light. Tiny at first, just a speck of splendor, it seemed to be traveling eastward. This star, new to the night sky, would not have been noticed unless one had been awake, looking upward, watching the stars sleepwalk across the skies. As it approached the constellation Orion directly overhead, the star grew in brightness, increasing in size and splendor. As it passed through Orion, now tiptoeing through the center of the night sky, the star began to speak to the sleepy world below. From the midst of their slumber people were awakened, not by any sound or movement, but by a strange feeling! Rubbing their eyes and looking skyward, they saw the new star with a trail of sparkling light flowing out behind it. Rich and poor, learned and uneducated, old and young, they all heard its silver voice — not with their ears, as one usually hears — for the message of the star gently massaged their hearts and said, "Come, follow me."

Now, in the center of the city there stood a tall

and mysterious tower, and at the top of this tower there were three priestly magi — scholars and astronomers — who were watching the night skies.

"Look," cried the youngest of the magi, "it is *the* Star!"

"Yes," acknowledged the woman magician, "it is the one for which we have waited."

"Come quickly," implored the third and oldest of the magi, "let us prepare at once to follow it."

Below the tower the city became filled with activity as people began to gather supplies for the journey. Excitement and adventure flooded the hearts of the people that night — but not everyone, for some objected, saying, "It is silly to leave at this hour. Let us wait 'til morning. Then in the full light of day we can examine this strange event. 'Tis perhaps only a bit of undigested beef!" Yet others objected, "We cannot *all* go; there are duties here. Who will clean and care for the temples and shrines? Who will guard their holy treasures if we all go after the Star? No, we will stay behind and care for the temples and keep the ancient times of incense while you others go."

Soon a great and colorful procession, accompanied by rousing music and banners flying in the wind, marched forth from the city gates, the pilgrims' torches of yellow and red flames illuminating the darkness of night. And so, the great pilgrimage of the Star began.

With the coming of dawn each day they stopped and rested; by night they traveled, following the wondrous Star with its long fan-shaped tail of beautiful, sparkling light. Ever eastward it led them as the days grew into weeks, the weeks into months, and the months into years.

Gradually problems and discontent arose among the pilgrims. Some began to grumble and to object,

"Surely, the Star did not intend for us to travel continuously!"

"Yes, you are right"; chimed in others, "we must have misunderstood its message." Many were plainly homesick; they longed for the temples and the comfort and security they afforded. So a delegation of these "concerned pilgrims" demanded a meeting. Many of the travelers were delighted at this — at long last something concrete was to be done. As a result of the meeting, committees were formed, and these were divided into discussion groups. Elections followed to appoint committee leaders. It was agreed by each of the committees that they should continue to follow the Star with the provision that weekly meetings of all committees be held.

As the meetings multiplied, sub-committees and review committees were added, and the business of organizing and attending them required so much energy that bit by bit people forgot about the Star. In time the committees determined by election that they had come "far enough." It was time to "stop and settle down." Plans were drawn up for temples which were very much like the ones they had left in their homeland. So great was their homesickness that many other things of the past were reinstituted as necessary and important for Star-followers. While all this was taking place, another small group of the caravan also held a meeting. These few were upset by the decision to stop and settle down. "The others have lost sight of the Star; they no longer hear its voice," said one. Another added, "Yes, they have a new star; it's called the meeting! They will never travel on much beyond this place."

"Come," said the woman magician, "we must continue to follow the Star. We must continue to follow this sacred messenger wherever it leads us."

And so, that night, a small party of the original

15

procession left the encampment where foundations
for the new temples had already been laid. They continued to travel eastward, following the wondrous
Star. Months continued to stretch into years, but still
they traveled onward. The youngest of the magi
watched, perhaps more closely than the rest, as one
by one even this last group of pilgrims began to drop
off until only the three magi were left. As they rode
along, the desert sand blowing in their faces, he could
not help but realize how disappointed and depressed
he had become. He remembered how he had been
electrified that night on the tower when the Star had
first appeared. He had been delighted and excited by
the prospect of the adventure. New places and strange
experiences were rich fare to him, and the fame and
glory of such an adventure had fueled his courage and
made the early difficulties seem unimportant. But as
the journey extended into years, he became increas-
ingly disillusioned. There was much hard work to the
journey, and its hardships — like the constant desert
wind and long hours in the saddle, not to mention the
constant bickering over little things — had emptied
him completely. On one particularly hot day he
stopped and said to the other two magi, "I'm tired of
this broken dream; I'm going home!"

The older magician encouraged him, "You can't
go home, my friend, once you have begun to follow a
star. You can never go home to that which is warm,
secure and unchanging, for when you arrive you
discover that it isn't home any more. No, for you the
road is your only home! Come, take heart — home
must be created wherever you are. Come, it is again
time to follow the Star!"

And so with renewed determination they rode on,
each of the magi lost in thought. The woman magician reflected to herself, "Life is not to be found in
temples nor in times of incense and prayer; life is

16

found only in following some 'unreachable' star. This journey may never end; people will not surrender their lives, their property and their hearts for dreams that are within easy reach. No," she thought, "only stars beyond one's grasp are truly worthy of total surrender; only such stars truly give life."

The oldest of the magi also rode on in silence, lost in his thoughts. He was a realist and understood that what they sought at the foot of the Star — at the end of the journey — did not exist. For years now they had followed the Star, sought the Mystic Bethlehem, yet they had never found it or any trace of it, this star-studded Shangri-La. The image of the manger, with ultimate security and motherly warmth, angels singing sweetly in the night air, friends and enemies united in peace and love — no such Bethlehem exists. He knew that they would *never* find it, because it exists only in dreams or in the hearts of romantics. Yet, he traveled doggedly onward, hypnotized by the splendor of that strange and beautiful Star.

Fifteen years had passed since the Star had first streaked across the night sky, and the three had left their tower. They had traveled countless roads and crossed many countries, and many of those who traveled with them had perished or given up the journey without finding where the Star was leading them — or even a reason for following it. The three were no closer now, it seemed, to finding the Mystery than on the day when they had begun their pilgrimage. No newfound Emmanuel, no glorious new age — only exhausted hearts and broken dreams.

Then, one night, it all came to an end — for the Star disappeared from the night sky! In the darkness without the Star to guide them, the journey of the three magi came to a sudden halt. Completely frustrated, they found themselves at the center of a wretched little village. While the other two magi were

17

lost in sorrow, the woman magician spoke up, "It is no use; we cannot go any further — the journey of the Star is ended." And the other two knew she was right. In silence they nodded their heads in agreement and slowly began to turn their camels around toward the way from which they had come.

However, the people of the village, poor and dirty, came out to see these illustrious visitors. Old and young, they crowded around the magi, begging food and money. The magi looked at one another and smiled. "Why not?" they thought as if in unison. "The pilgrimage is finished." And so they emptied their saddle bags of their remaining provisions and handed out the precious gifts they had carried all these years to the ragged, dirty villagers. As they did, the youngest of the magi began to lift children up onto his camel, giving them rides around the village square. The magi were so involved in giving away their possessions and entertaining the children that they failed to see that the wondrous Star had reappeared! It was, however, no longer moving eastward — rather, now it was suspended *directly over* the magi. And from the Star, glory was streaking downward in a great shower of sparkling light.

The magi never found Christmas —
the magi had *become* Christmas!

"That's a most interesting story. I will have to reflect on all its implications,"* I said. "And you were
right; as you spoke I felt that every part of me was
absorbed in your story. I felt that I was on that journey myself."

The Ethiopian smiled as he poured me a small
cup of thick black coffee. "Good, and if you are in
no great hurry, I have other stories."

"Please," I replied, "I would love to hear them."
As I sipped my coffee, he began . . .

---

*For the author's reflections on each of the parables, see the section
beginning on page 168.

The Refugees

Once upon a time in a distant land, there was a majestic castle-city built high atop a mountain. Many were its tall, flag-topped towers; massive its high, grey walls which rose upward steeply from the slopes of the mountain. Winding past this castle-city was a great highway that ran the full length of the country. Every day of late, the highway had been crowded, from edge to edge, with a ragtag army of refugees. Each day, ranks of these refugees would tread past the castle carrying their few meager possessions, their eyes downcast and their hearts empty of hope. They came from all levels of society — the highly educated and the uneducated, the rich as well as the poor. They were, all of them, victims of the Great Disturbance, and now the road was their only home. They were, as are all refugees, people of great want, people who had suffered great loss, and yet no country or kingdom wanted them. For, indeed, did not each country have its own poor and unemployed, its destitute — and who, indeed, had need of any more problems? And so the refugees wandered, without hope.

One day, rather late in the afternoon, a man and his wife left the moving masses of refugees on the highway in order to climb up a narrow, twisting road that led to the castle-city on the mountain. As they did so, their friends who remained on the highway shouted after them, " 'Tis only a waste of time, friends; this castle is no different from any of the others. They'll not open their gates to you nor offer you any help. We are the homeless, the aliens, and no doors open in welcome to us."

But the man and his wife did not give heed to their voices, for a tiny wick of hope flickered, if only very faintly, in their hearts. With difficulty and great apprehension the couple finally arrived at the tall, iron gates of the castle. They knocked and waited. Presently, a small, barred window in one of the gates opened and a voice asked, "Do you have an appointment?"

"No," replied the man.

"Then," returned the voice, "what do you want?"

"We seek the Prince," answered the man. "We are in great need and have come in response to his invitation."

"I am a personal servant of the Great Prince," came the reply. "You say you are in need — but are you citizens of this castle-city? If you will kindly show me your identification papers, I will open the gates to you. As I said, I have the honor of being the servant and personal representative of the Prince."

"We have no identification papers, venerable servant of the Prince," answered the refugee. "We were — or rather are — his faithful subjects, but we have been uprooted and cast out from our home by the Great Disturbance. The times, sir, as you well know, are most difficult: war, revolution, famine, and unrest everywhere."

His wife, her very body proclaiming hunger and great weariness, added, "Please, sir, can't we come in for just a moment? It has been a long, hard climb for us to reach your gates."

"Well," answered the servant at the gate, "since you are subjects of the Prince . . . " And the massive, iron gates slowly swung open just barely enough to allow them to enter. They were ushered into a small, dark gateroom by the servant, a heavy-set man who wore a luxurious, flowing fur robe. The room was

21

rather stark, containing only a table, a few chairs and some large, legal-looking ledgers that filled the top of the table. On one wall, however, lending some character to the room, was a single picture in a large golden frame. The image in the picture was of a man with kind eyes and a friendly countenance.

"Yes, yes," said the servant, his voice dripping with dullness, "can't we be quick about this? I'm a busy man. I have numerous duties to perform as the official representative of the Prince," he said, pointing to the picture on the wall. "There is the ringing of bells and the raising of flags at appointed hours, meetings to attend, and of course I have many official forms to fill out. So, what is it, my good man, what can I do for you?"

"We have come to ask . . . to see if it is possible . . . er . . . a," answered the man in a hesitant voice, "we have need of . . . "

"Well, let us see," interrupted the plump servant as he picked up a large, grey ledger, "are your names listed in the census? Are your taxes properly paid? Have you or your wife ever been on one of the numerous castle committees?"

"NO!" answered the wife, "It is as my husband has said; we are refugees. But we are also loyal subjects of the Prince. We have come here because we have always been told that our beloved Prince said, 'Let all who are in need come to me.' Is this not one of his castles?"

"Yes, yes," muttered the servant as he softly stroked the sleeve of his fur robe. "True, true, my good woman, but life is not always that simple. There are regulations and laws, all made in the name of the Prince and for the common good. There are forms to be filled out, classes to be attended, and of course . . ." and here he smiled at them, "the question of your unpaid taxes. Shall we take care of these first and then

22

see to your needs?"

Then, looking at his large, gold watch he let out a theatrical gasp and said, "Oh, my, my, look at what time it is already! I am sorry, but you folks will have to come back tomorrow. It is sunset, and I have duties to perform, matters of grave consequence to attend to. I am sorry, but I didn't make the laws. I'm sure you understand. So sorry — good night now, and God bless you." And with a flourish of his flowing robes he quickly ushered them out of the front gate.

Already night was wrapping the countryside in its twilight, turquoise shawl as the man and his wife, with heavy hearts and leaden steps, made their way back to the highway. All along the sides of the highway small campfires flickered as the refugees huddled together and shared with one another their meager rations of food. The flames licked away the chilling darkness, and families spoke to one another about happier times, before the Great Disturbance had cast them from their homes. As the moon rose behind the mountain, the castle was silhouetted by its pale, white light. The warm lights of its windows dotted the castle's silent, dark shape. The refugees looked up, and each of them was reminded of the castle-city that had once been home. But this one, like all the others along the highway, was not to become a new home.

Suddenly, however, the depression of their homesickness was lifted as the music of some stringed instrument floated across the night air. Before long a soft but strong voice began to sing, "Come to me, all you who are in need . . . and I will help you." Slowly, the ragged refugees gathered around the stranger who played and sang. His tattered cloak and battered hat were as threadbare as their own clothing. A sudden gust of wind fanned the fire, sparks swirled upward in a golden cloud, and a circle of light and warmth

23

burst outward, illuminating the faces of all. The woman who had climbed up to the castle tugged at her husband's arm and whispered, "I've seen his face before, but where?" Gently taking her hand the man said, "The face is the same as the one in the picture . . . on the wall of the gatehouse in the castle!"

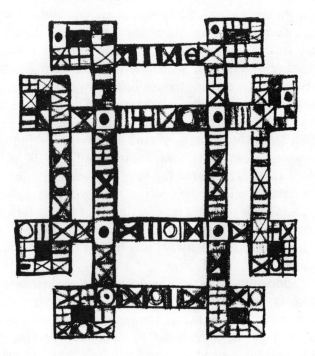

The Cobbler

Once, a long, long time ago, there existed at the foot of a great range of mountains a beautiful and peaceful kingdom. Rising sharply from a vast green plain, the tall and majestic mountains stood from horizon to horizon. Covered with great, white glaciers and beautiful snowcapped peaks, they towered silently above the green forests and gently rolling farmland. The people who lived in the countless tiny villages scattered across the kingdom called the high range of mountains the "Great White Giants."

In almost any cottage of every village one could find a picture of the King. Each year the people of this land would, on the occasion of the King's birthday, celebrate their most colorful festival. But, except for his picture, no one had ever seen the King! When the village elders were asked by the children, "Where does the King live?" they would point toward the tall mountain peaks and say, "Our King lives in a hidden valley beyond the Great White Giants." Naturally, as you might guess, there were among the people of the kingdom those who doubted the existence of such a place as the hidden valley or even that there was a King! But their number was few, and they usually kept their theories to themselves.

The villages of the kingdom that dotted the vast expanses of green land at the base of the Great White Giants were composed of small, white cottages and narrow, crooked lanes. In one of these villages, down one of these crooked lanes, there lived a cobbler. As he repaired run-down heels or patched worn-out soles, he would dream of a great adventure. His long-

25

ing was to go out one day in search of the King. He yearned, with a great passion, to see the face of the King. One day, he put away his tools, closed the door of his shoe shop and slipped away. He said nothing to his family or friends but simply left. Why worry them, he thought, for he was aware that no one had ever crossed the Great White Giants and returned to tell about it. Those who had even attempted to climb them had returned after a few days with horrible stories about the dangers of such an impossible feat.

With a small canvas bag of supplies strapped to his back, the cobbler began the steep upward climb toward the vast, windswept glacier slopes which took up where the trees ended. As he trudged across the enormous expanse of snow and ice, the bitterly cold winds would push him backwards but were unable to keep him from plodding on. The higher he climbed the more he was surrounded by dense fog and clouds. The harsh winds, now filled with needles of ice, tore at his clothing and blinded his vision. He staggered onward, nevertheless, always onward toward his destination. Reality and fantasy blended in the grey, silent world of swirling clouds and snow, but he held tightly to his dream of seeing the face of the King. Although everything in nature seemed opposed to his efforts, that yearning in his heart was a singular beacon calling him ever forward.

One day, or was it night — he knew not the difference by now — half-frozen and ready to drop from exhaustion, he discovered a narrow canyon in the towering crystal walls of ice. That narrow passageway led out into the brilliant sunlight. The reflection of the sun off the ice momentarily blinded him as he found himself on the edge of a glacier cliff. Below he could see a beautiful, lush, green valley. The sounds of bird-song, running water and some strange but soft

26

strains of music drifted upward from the valley. He stood there, unbelieving, his head reeling — and then, in a mixture of joy and fatigue, he collapsed.

When he awoke much later, he found himself in a great and ornate palace. His ragged and tattered clothing was gone. His body had been bathed and annointed with scented oils, and he was lying on a large, soft bed. Scores of servants in long flowing robes stood around the bed, ready to assist him. They told the cobbler that he had been discovered unconscious by shepherds and brought to the palace. As he marveled at this wonderful story and at his glorious surroundings, they also told him that he was to dine, that very night, with the Great King himself.

Dressed in a magnificent golden robe, the cobbler was seated at table next to the King. As he relished in the great riches of the feast and in the singular attention that the King was lavishing upon him, the King spoke to the cobbler of his affection for him and for all the people of the kingdom. The King said that he planned, soon, to come and visit his kingdom. He told the cobbler that upon his return home he was to tell all the people of the King's great affection for them. The feast lasted long into the night, and throughout the remarkable affair the King revealed to the cobbler many wondrous and mysterious things. Then as the last lamps were flickering out the King gave the cobbler a sparkling, jeweled ring from his own finger. The ring flashed with ice-blue fire as the King said, "This will be a sign that you and I are friends and that you have indeed feasted with me."

The next day, wearing the jeweled ring and robed in the splendorous, golden garments of the palace, the little cobbler left the hidden valley, escorted by the King's own attendants. When they reached the great glacier at the rim of the mountain peaks, the very place where the hidden canyon entrance was located,

27

the attendants said farewell, since that was as far as they could go. The cobbler warmly waved good-bye, turned away and entered the ice canyon for his difficult journey across the Great White Giants toward his home.

Once again the fierce mountain winds savagely slashed at him with razor-like fingers. Day followed upon day as he blindly stumbled through the vast, empty, silent wasteland of snow and ice. Again, near exhaustion as he inched his way homeward, he suddenly saw patches of blue sky through a window in the fog and clouds. The hazy window opened and closed, and through it he could look clearly below to his green homeland at the foot of the towering peaks. His face was leathered by the freezing wind, and his once glorious garments were reduced to tattered, grey rags. Looking down at his hands he was shocked to see that the gift-ring from the King was missing. It must have slipped from his finger somewhere back in that wasteland of snow and fog. Battered, half-frozen and resembling some ragged beggar, he descended the mountains and once again set foot in his home village.

His family, close friends and a crowd of villagers encircled him as he related to them the adventures of his pilgrimage. Although he now lacked any visible proof of his visit to the King, there was about the cobbler something very different. A special attitude — perhaps it was an inner power or light — made him a different man. It was this something "extra," this sense of aliveness, that was a sign to his friends that the cobbler's story was indeed true. Nevertheless, not everyone believed him. Some maintained that it was only snow-shock that brought about his story, that his adventure was all a fantasy or that he was insane. Still, many would crowd into his small shoe shop to hear him tell the story. It wasn't what the cobbler

28

said that was important — though the story was indeed interesting — it was the cobbler himself that was the message! From his eyes there flowed a radiance that shone with the brilliance of ice-blue fire. In his presence one could feel that "extra" something; it was good, it was beautiful, and it was, most of all, *alive*.

Over and over, to all who asked, he would tell the story. Casual friends became constant companions and even came to live with him. They urged the cobbler to let his story be carried to the other villages in the kingdom. By now countless visitors from far away were coming to his shoe shop to hear him and be near him. To many he would also give encouragement to travel across the silent wastelands of glaciers to visit the King. He would say to them, "It *is* possible, friends; even I, a simple cobbler, have done it!" "But, good cobbler," they would protest, "we have families and farms to care for; we cannot go off climbing distant mountains in search of hidden canyons that do not exist on maps or charts!" They did not mention the fear they felt about the dangers and privations of the journey. Others exclaimed, "Surely there must be another way; tell us, good cobbler!" To those he felt were sincere and ready, the cobbler confided one of the secrets given him by the King — that the King himself would come to them instead of their coming to him! "Go home and close your door; go into your room and be very, very still," said the cobbler. "Follow your inner beacon, and you will find the hidden passageway. Wait patiently at the end of it . . . the King will come to you!" Soon those who lived with the cobbler also began to radiate this special extra-aliveness.

The number of the cobbler's friends continued to grow. Many of the newer ones urged that some way be found for the message to be spread across all the kingdom, even to its most remote corners. One day, a group of them rushed to the cobbler, who was by now quite aged and no longer well, and told him, "A wise man in one of our distant villages has discovered a new science called radiotelegraphy. It is the science of communicating over great distances by converting sounds into electromagnetic waves, transmitting them directly through space without connecting wires to a receiver set, which then changes them back into sounds." The friends of the cobbler jumped up and down with glee, for surely this was an answer to their prayers. Now the message of the cobbler would not be lost but might be spread across all the land. But radiotelegraphy was too big a word for the simple people of the villages, so they simply shortened it to "ra-di-o."

The old cobbler agreed to the plan but insisted that the secret message of how to possess that extra-aliveness must accompany the story. Seeming to hear only the cobbler's approval, however faint, an enormous amount of activity followed from this group of friends. Workers began to construct a great power plant and transformer. On the top of this large building was a tall, spiral structure called a broad-casting tower. Others were building small black boxes which were to be the receiving sets for the electro-magnetic waves. Men were trained in special schools for long years as technicians in order to operate all the new and complicated equipment. A company for broadcasting was founded with a president and a board of directors. They, in turn, ordered the training of men to operate and maintain the little black boxes that were to be sent to each village. One such repre-sentative of the Broadcasting Company was sent to every village of the great kingdom. The organization of such an effort required great coordination, and so there was a need for district and regional supervisors and assistant supervisors, as well as for inspectors and instructors. Each village was responsible for constructing its own special building to house the black box, the "ra-di-o." This building was called by the people the "House of the Message." It usually was the most beautiful and the largest building in the entire village and could be easily recognized by the tall, spiral broadcasting tower that stood on its roof.

Each week on the appointed day all the people of the village — men, women and children — would gather in the House of the Message. When they were all present, the representative of the Broadcasting Company, called the "ra-di-o man," would enter dressed as a cobbler. All would stand and sing a song about the King or sometimes about the cobbler or his friends. Following the song the ra-di-o man would speak about the financial problems of broadcasting and the need for sacrifice. On other days he might speak about the great need for young men to become technicians of the Broadcasting Company. Then the solemn moment came, the one that everyone had been waiting for: the time of the message. With great ritual, the ra-di-o man would turn on the little black box. As the electrical tubes warmed up and turned bright orange, the people would sit in hushed silence. But instead of a message all that could be heard was an electric hum broken by an occasional crackle of static. After perhaps fifteen minutes of this humming and static, the ra-di-o man would, with great ceremony, turn off the ra-di-o. All would then stand and sing another song. The ceremony thus ended, the people would visit with one another for a time on the steps of the House of the Message and then go home to dinner.

Now, while taking into account that the ritual of the ra-di-o was quite beautiful, that the songs were pleasant, and even the fact that the House of the

31

Message was most artistic and attractive; for the most part, no one ever thought to say, "But there was no message, nothing is being broadcast!" Yet when small children, who innocently speak the truth, would ask their parents if they could stay home and play since nothing happened at the House of the Message, the parents would respond, "But the cobbler, before he died, told us to listen to the message, that it would tell us how we might have the extra-aliveness that he had. The important thing, children, is to be present for the ritual of turning on and turning off the ra-di-o. After all, it's only an hour; surely you can spare that much time from your play."

Most of the parents suspected, but never told their children, that those who worked for the Broadcasting Company themselves did not know the message. They had been so busy with the machinery of the transmitter and with the complicated ritual of the ra-di-o that they had either forgotten the message or, in the confusion, had never learned it.

Indeed, these employees did know the story of the cobbler. In fact, the Broadcasting Company had learned experts who knew the most detailed and most interesting facts about "the story." And there were others whose business it was to write the laws that seemed to flow from the story. Actually, there were two major camps of opinion in the Broadcasting Company: those who held that knowledge of the story was most important and those who held that the behavior of the people who went to the House of the Message was central. It was the sole work of this second group to invent new laws. To be sure, those of the Broadcasting Company did possess the story of the cobbler; it was all written down in books. But the words of these volumes and volumes by themselves were dead; it was the cobbler who had been really alive.

As the years passed by, more and more people stopped coming to the House of the Message. On the special day of the gathering, they would spend the morning in bed or would even go fishing. These activities did not give them that extra-aliveness either, but at least they were not as dull as listening to that electric emptiness when attending the House of the Message.

One day, in a small cottage down a narrow twisting lane, there was a seamstress who made a decision. Her work was the mending of dresses and the patching of worn-out clothing. As she worked at her sewing, she would dream of seeing the face of the King. This desire had been growing for a long time, and on this particular day she knew that the time had come. So she put away her scissors and thread, closed the door to her shop, and slipped away without telling her family or friends. A small brown pack was strapped to her shoulders as she followed the road out of the village, past the House of the Message. Then, turning northward, she headed for the Great White Giants.

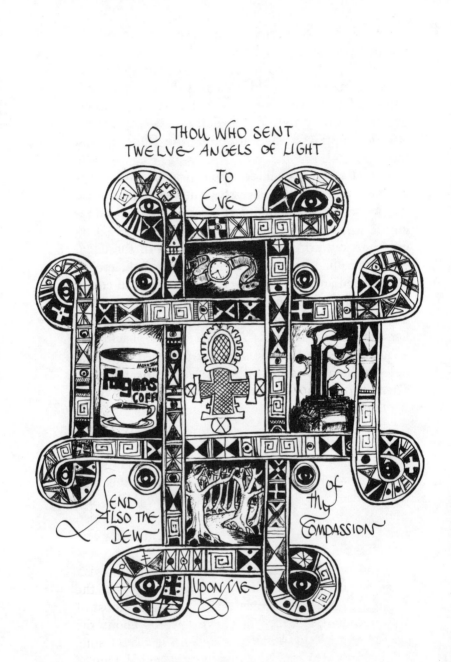

Smiley

Smiley was a most happy fellow. Each day his heart would overflow with happiness; he simply radiated it. Even his pockets were filled with joy. This gift of happiness he freely shared with one and all. Now, for Smiley — folks had given him the name because he always had a warm, generous smile on his face — every day was the best day of his life. And, as he would say, "Why not?" That was Smiley's favorite response to those who would question him about how it was possible to be happy at all times. "Why shouldn't I be happy?" he would say, "I have all that I need for happiness: *I'm alive*."

One day, as he was on a journey that took him through a great forest, he came upon two strangers seated on a fallen old tree that rested beside the winding forest road. To the ordinary person the two men might have looked suspicious and strangely out of place, for they wore unusual, out-of-date western wear, complete with wide-brimmed hats and cowboy boots. Most people would have looked the other way and hurried on by them as they passed. But not Smiley. To Smiley the word "stranger" did not exist. For him there were only friends, those he knew and those he had not yet met.

And so, quite naturally, Smiley stopped to visit with them. He chatted on about the beauty of the day, not seeming to notice that it had rained most of the morning. He spoke in glowing words about the beauty of the forest and how delightful was the song of the birds. The strangers nodded and smiled. One of them, the older of the two, asked Smiley if they

35

might accompany him on the road since they also were traveling in the same direction and had only stopped to rest for a moment. Smiley was delighted at the suggestion, and so the three took to the winding forest road.

The older of the two strangers said, "My name is Frank, what's yours?"

"My name is Smiley — at least that's what folks call me," he answered.

"Nice name," replied the stranger. "And where are you headed, Smiley?"

"For the next village; it's at the other side of the forest. Beautiful place, I would guess, if it borders on such a grand forest," replied Smiley.

Frank frowned, saying, "Where are you going to stay when you get there, Smiley? I understand that rooms there are hard to find. And what kind of work will you do? I understand that there's lots of unemployment, not to mention that the town folks hate strangers."

Smiley didn't speak at first, lost in thought. "I guess I just hadn't thought about those things. But now that you mention it, I should be concerned." Smiley walked on in silence as he reflected about where he would stay, what he would do and how people would receive him. In fact, he was so preoccupied with his thoughts that he didn't notice that Frank, the stranger on his left, was at that very moment picking his pocket — emptying it of happiness.

Frank, having picked Smiley's pocket, winked at the man who walked on Smiley's right side. As if picking up on a well-rehearsed secret sign, he asked, "And where did you come from, Smiley?"

The question brought Smiley out of his deep thought, and he answered with a broad smile. "From the beautiful little town back there on the other side of the forest. Wonderful place, filled with friendly people."

"Nice people, huh?" asked the stranger.

"Oh, yes," replied Smiley, "they were all so kind and good to me."

"But how did you feel when some of them — surely *some* of them — must have figured that you were a little crazy to be happy all the time? Didn't it bother you that some people thought you were a little simple? And your family, what did they think?"

"To tell the truth," said Smiley, "none of that ever occurred to me before. Yeah, I guess some of them did treat me like I was simple. They grinned a lot and probably laughed at me behind my back. And my dad, well, he always said that I wouldn't amount to much . . . . " Here Smiley's voice trailed off, and he became lost in memories of his childhood and his experiences in the town from which he had just come. In fact, Smiley was so lost in his memories that he was unaware that the stranger who walked on his right side was even then picking his pocket — removing all the happiness that was contained there.

With a clever toss of the head, Frank winked at the other man in a way that Smiley couldn't see, and they both reached in and picked clean the pockets of his heart, stripping them bare of happiness.

Smiley was now no longer smiling but was lost in thoughts of the future and the past. When the three came to a fork in the road Frank slapped him on the back and said, "Well, good friend, here is where we must part company; we're taking this other road. Best of luck up ahead in that unfriendly village; hope you can find some decent work to do." And the other man added, "Yeah, I hope the people are better and more friendly than those in the town you just came from."

"Thanks," answered Smiley. "I've appreciated

37

your company and all your suggestions and advice. It was nice meetin' you. But I didn't catch the name of your friend, Frank."

"That's my kid brother," returned Frank, his face aglow with pride. "His name is Jessie. Folks call us the James Boys!"

"The James Boys?" replied Smiley. "You mean the famous train robbers?"

"No," answered Jessie, "we stopped holding up trains long ago. We're after much more precious loot these days. Now they call us 'The Time Bandits!'"

The New God

In the beginning, all creation worshipped only God the Creator as the Lord of Life. The Creator, who could have demanded any number of impressive titles, preferred simply to be called "God." For billions of years, if not longer, God was the only god that existed. Life was simple then, and there was only one commandment: "Love God and one another." God believed that if this one commandment were observed then everything else that was needed would happen — by a sort of spontaneous chain reaction.

Many centuries after the creation of man and woman another god appeared on earth. He insisted on being called "the Only True God" and had his special commandment: "You shall have no other gods before Me; I alone shall you worship." God the Creator did not much care for this new god, and the Only True God was jealous of the Creator.

God the Creator had some shrines and temples built in his honor by human hands. They were nice but not nearly as beautiful as the ones that he had built himself. Being an artist, God loved to build his own shrines. Since he was so creative, he enjoyed using as many different kinds of materials to build them as his godly imagination could conceive. The new deity, on the other hand, did not build his own shrines. His monuments were built by his disciples who also maintained them and kept them in good working order. In the beginning only the chosen few enjoyed his shrines and worshipped him — priests and kings and the like. But gradually belief in the new lord spread, and soon sailors, merchants and even

common folk worshipped him. The sacred image of
the Only True God was soon in nearly every home,
and sometimes in every room of the home. The truly
devoted, who amounted to just about everyone (at
least in the busy and industrious parts of the world)
carried a small private shrine of the new god on their
very person.

Now while the shrines to the new deity were
nearly everywhere, there was one place where they
were not. They were not to be seen in the shrines that
God the Creator had built by his own hands. It was in
one of these beautiful and holy shrines that our story
really begins.

High in the mountains, in an untamed part of the
land where the snow line creeps down to gently caress
the green fir trees, there lived a handsome young man
whose name was Tim. Considered a heathen, a pagan,
Tim was mistrusted by those who knew him because
he neither believed in nor worshipped the Only True
God. Tim's neighbors, like most of the people on
earth, were convinced that only by having no other
gods but the Only True God could anyone be saved.
If one did not believe in him, bow to him frequently
during the day and keep his shrine — preferably on
one's very person — it would mean damnation!

Tim did not believe, nor did he have a personal
shrine, and so he was viewed as strange, if not eccen-
tric, by those who lived in the village at the foot of
the mountain. The Only True God, as everyone
acknowledged, was the source of life and success. He
determined all the actions of people, from their rising
and going to bed to their comings and goings. He
determined the limits of their work and play and even
stood watch over their love-making. Oh, he was indeed the Mightiest Lord God in all the universe.

Now one day when Tim had come down to the
village, he saw a beautiful girl named Kathleen.

40

Struck by her charming beauty, he invited her to come and visit him where he lived, high in the cloud-capped moutains. Delighted, she rushed home with news of the invitation, but her mother said, "Kathleen, dear, I know that he's handsome and that there are few young men, handsome or not, in our little village. But, dear, he's not of our faith. He's more than an unbeliever, he's a heathen. Only trouble awaits you if you fall in love with such as him. Marry a believer, one of your own." Kathleen's mother was a woman wise in the ways of the world who knew that to marry outside one's religion was only to invite hardship into one's life. But, like most young girls, Kathleen didn't listen to her mother's advice; she climbed the mountain to visit Tim.

Upon her arrival Tim suggested that they have a picnic beside a crystal clear lake surrounded by towering green fir trees. The picnic was marvelous. Together they talked and shared dreams. Tim spoke of the beauty of the seasons, of sunsets and sunrises, as flights of butterflies circled lazily overhead in the clear blue mountain sky. Suddenly Kathleen bowed and prayed to the Only True God. The prayer was brief; it took only a second or two, but it was long enough for Tim to become angry.

"What the hell!" he said. "Can't we ever be out of the sight of your damn god? What a stupid time to pray to him!"

"Oh, Tim," cried Kathleen, "be careful; you musn't say that sort of thing out loud. You might be struck down by the hand of the Only True God! Don't be angry; I promise I'll not pray again while we are together."

"Kathleen, I don't mind if you pray"; said Tim, "it's to whom you pray that makes me angry. Your god is an uncaring and ruthless god. And those who worship him lead cramped and un-free lives. Night

41

and day they are prisoners of him and his devotions. Whenever they are having a good time, as you are here, what do they do? They pray their little devotions and surrender to his unholy will. And when they do, all the magic and wonder evaporates from their lives. Kathleen, pray to God but not to the Only True God. Worship *my* God and you will never have to pause for prayer when you are in the middle of something you really enjoy. In fact, whenever you do not acknowledge the Only True God but are totally absorbed in whatever you're doing, that in itself is prayer to my God. Please be my wife, for I love you. Leave your religion and join mine. Worship my God and I promise you enjoyment like you have never known. I promise you freedom and . . . "

"Oh, Tim," wept Kathleen, "I so want to love you and let your God become my God. But I'm afraid that if I do I'll be damned."

"No," said Tim tenderly, taking her into his arms. "No . . . no . . . it's the followers of the Only True God who have damned themselves, in this life and the next. Trust me." As he kissed her, her heart exploded with freedom and joy. And she knew that Tim was right, that what he had said was the truth. And so to Tim's delight she slowly removed her sacred image of the Only True God, the image she had worn with devotion since she was a young girl, and she threw it into the mountain lake. Her personal shrine sank slowly with a quiet gurgle. Soon the two lovers were married, and they lived happily ever after, as sweethearts in all good stories do.

Even to this day, if you should go to a certain grey rock ledge, beside a certain blue lake at the foot of a certain tall mountain and look deep down into the crystal waters, you will see, lying at the bottom of the lake, the rusty image of the Only True God. The round face is faded, the numbers dim, and the

42

hands are bent and twisted. Its band will never im-
prison an arm again, and the heartbeat of the shrine
which once held the power to rule a life is silenced.

The Magic Folger's Coffee Can

The little blond-haired boy was lost in another world as he walked along the winding creek, following a wooden stick that rode the gentle current of the small stream. To the boy the brown stick was not the small broken branch that others might see. Rather, it was a sailing ship and he, its captain. Lost in the adventure of sailing down a great river in some far-off land, the small boy was unaware that the creek was about to bend under an old, wooden country bridge.

As he passed under the bridge, the coolness and darkness of the shade created by the bridge overhead woke him again to who and where he was. But there was something more than just the shade that caused him to forget about his adventures as a captain on an imaginary ship. He stood there under the bridge, his eyes growing accustomed to the sudden change from the bright sunlight, aware that something or someone was present.

He looked up to the place where the bridge's timbers met the bank of the creek and could see in the darkness two small, bright lights. As his eyes became acclimated to the shade and shadows, he could see that the two lights were actually eyes and that they belonged to a tiny old man — or at least something that looked like a man! In reality, it was a troll with the most marvelously flaming-bright, twinkling eyes you could imagine. He wore a wide and generous smile and said to the boy, "You look very, very happy, young man."

44

"I am. I'm having a lot of fun now that it's summer and we don't have school. But you . . . you look even happier. You look like the happiest person I have ever seen in my whole life," replied the blond-headed boy, his voice full of admiration.

"Well," answered the troll, "I am very happy, but more than that I know the secret of happiness. Would you like me to gift you with that secret, young man?"

"Oh, yes!" said the boy, eager for such a treasure, eager to be as happy as the funny old man who sat with such contentment under the old wooden bridge.

" 'Tis easy," replied the troll, and from an old, brown gunny sack beside him he produced an object and tossed it to the boy. "Here, this is a gift to you. It is a magic Folger's Coffee Can — fill it to the brim and you will be happy always."

With great excitement the little boy caught the red Folger's Coffee Can which the troll had thrown to him. With a few hurried words of gratitude he rushed off for home, intent on filling his magic Folger's Coffee Can to the brim.

On arriving at home he ran to his bedroom and began stuffing the coffee can with his toys — his baseball glove, his stamp collection, his toy cars . . . and thus began, so very innocently, a lifetime passion.

As he grew older and entered high school, he stuffed the top grades in his class, football and baseball trophies and various other honors into his Folger's Coffee Can. Yet for some reason the can never became full, full to the brim. He raced on in life, anxious to taste the happiness promised by the old troll under the bridge. In college he again added top grades, more intellectual awards, more athletic honors. He became the president of his class and of several social and academic groups. He was voted "the most likely to be a success" and eagerly pushed that

45

honor into his magic can. But for some reason, although each of these prizes had a very sweet taste, the coffee can never seemed to be really full.

Besides honors and high grades the blond-headed, good-looking, athletic young man also stuffed good times, good food and drink, the attention and affection of beautiful women and of many friends into his Folger's Coffee Can. After each rich experience he would feel very happy, and it would seem that his coffee can was full. But by the time he would wake up the next morning it was painfully clear that the Folger's can was not full to the brim.

Through his thirties, though he had a wife, children, three cars, a beautiful home, a successful career, and even two mistresses, he continued his personal obsession to fill the coffee can. He became head of his company, held great power and was respected by all, but he wasn't happy. The now old and dented, red Folger's Coffee Can sat on his desk in his walnut-paneled executive office. Every day he would stuff stocks, bonds, property and an ever-increasing parade of sensual pleasures into it, but it still wasn't enough.

His friends told him that he had a winning personality and all the right qualifications and that he should run for public office. So he did, and won the election easily. Into his Folger's Coffee Can he crammed all the respect, honor, authority and most of all the power of his elected office, but was sad to see that the coffee can was still not full.

Now in his old age, his skin wrinkled and brown-blotched with liver marks, his hair turned white and all but gone, he was making the final arrangements for the most gigantic of all international corporate deals. It would make him the most powerful and the richest man in the world. He signed the transaction papers and then walked to the window of his office that overlooked his vast corporate empire. With a wry smile he took the multinational conglomerate contract and began to stuff it greedily into his battered, old Folger's Coffee Can. At that very moment he was struck by a fatal heart attack. As he stumbled forward, the Folger's Coffee Can slipped from his hand and flew out the high office window.

When the coffee can hit the pavement it bounced high and freely into the air, almost as if it were glad to be out of the grasp of the rich, old man. With a sort of playfulness it bounced several more times and then rolled joyfully down the street past the tall office buildings. It rolled along, gathering speed, through the hectic business district, turned up a freeway ramp, and continued to speed along until it reached the edge of the great, noisy and bustling city.

The Folger's Coffee Can then rolled off an exit and turned down a street with trees and small, pleasant, one-storied, white frame houses. Slowing down now, it hopped the curb with one final, playful bounce and rolled to a stop in the middle of a green lawn where a little, blond-haired girl was in the midst of a tea party with three of her dolls and her set of tiny white and blue-rimmed china.

The little blond-haired girl picked up the can and looked at it inquisitively. She immediately noticed something that its previous owner, the richest man in the world, had never seen — had never taken the time to see because he was so busy trying to fill it.

The little, blond-haired girl was puzzled because the Folger's Coffee Can had no bottom in it! If its previous owner had ever stopped to look at his life, he would have seen a long trail of possessions, pleasures, honors and power that were left behind him. But the tunnel-like opening of the tin coffee can, unnoticed during the old man's whole life, delighted the little girl.

She held the can skyward, and it became filled with the golden sun. She held it up toward a bird, and it was filled not only with the beauty of the creature but with its lovely song as well. She filled it with her dolls as they sat in all properness at their front lawn tea party. She filled it with flowers and people, and running to a hallway mirror in her home she filled it with herself.

With delight she called out, "Oh, Mother, come quickly! A magic Folger's Coffee Can has just rolled into our yard. Come quickly, Mother; I'm the richest and happiest person in the world. The whole world, Mother, the whole world is in my red, magic Folger's Coffee Can."

The Mountain

Once, long ago and far from here, there existed a gigantic mountain. It had no specific name but was simply called "The Mountain." Perched on one side of this immense mountain was a city whose name was, as you might expect, "The City of the Mountain." Legends tell that in the beginning people worshipped the mountain as a God. Steam and hot water from the vast hidden underground pools gushed up through the rocks and heated their homes and cooked their food. Even after the people stopped worshipping it as God, the mountain continued to care for them, supplying heat, energy and even the food that grew on its fertile slopes.

About one hundred years ago, a huge factory was built on a hill outside the city (actually, the city was nestled in a saddle-like valley between two hills that formed one side of the mountain). The factory, which was over ten stories high, manufactured funeral wreaths. These wreaths, with their plastic flowers and artificial greens, were then shipped all over the world. Some time after the building of the factory, the name of the city was changed. From that time onward it was called Factoryville. Day and night the great factory rumbled with activity as its five tall smokestacks belched out huge clouds of grey soot.

Everyone who lived in Factoryville worked, in one way or another, for the funeral wreath factory. When the young came of age and thought about leaving home to seek their fortunes in the world, they did not leave. Like their parents they remained in Factoryville. To have a job at the factory was to have

49

security, and who knew what it might be like out there in the world? So they stayed. Their jobs had a purpose, and so life had meaning. After all, did not people need funeral wreaths to honor their dead and to decorate their tombs?

Like most industrial towns, however, the people who lived in Factoryville suffered from an occupational disease: boredom and depression! They were a cheerless and dispirited group. They seemed bogged down and at times even found it difficult to breathe. And even though in the beginning their work seemed to have purpose and meaning, for the great majority it no longer did. Although they had freely chosen to live and work in Factoryville, they now felt trapped in a valley of grey depression. Their lives all had narrow horizons and appeared to have no alternatives. Day after day they trudged up the hill to the factory, carrying their lunch pails — long, grey lines of workers, all of whom looked alike. Even their homes resembled one another. Block after block of small grey boxes with small square windows, one next to the other with no beauty or color — this was Factoryville.

Depression was not the only sickness of these people; they also suffered from a nagging guilt. They always seemed to feel guilty and often went to church for relief. After confessing that they felt guilty (not for anything in particular but just a general feeling), the voice of the old priest, with pious conviction, echoed across the church: "For your penance, my child, work overtime. Go now and you will find peace." And they did — as long as they continued to work long and hard. But the cure was an affliction that became an addiction. Seeking relief from their lingering guilt, the people worked harder and harder — extra hours and late into the night. Even on their days off they worked hard at home,

50

trimming the bushes or covering their homes with a fresh coat of grey paint. Every home had a front porch, but no one had time to sit and enjoy the sport of doing nothing. While the people of Factoryville were honest and decent, they never thought to themselves, "Why do we feel guilty? Why is it so painful to do nothing?"

Now, across town on the hill opposite the funeral wreath factory, there was a makeshift amusement park called Joyland. Originally it had been a carnival that came to town on tour, but because it lacked funds to move on, the carnival had to settle on the hill. Beneath the great roller coaster, called the Dragon's Tail, was a collection of lean-tos and old, rusted trailers in which lived the folks who worked at Joyland. In addition to the roller coaster the carnival also had a large ferris wheel, a merry-go-round and many other mechanical rides. Joyland also had a sideshow, or midway, whose major attraction was a wide variety of freaks from all parts of the world.

The strings of sparkling lights and colored flags of the amusement park were in sharp contrast to the ominous, great, dark factory that rose like a bastile on the opposite side of the city. Joyland, however, was the one form of entertainment the citizens of Factoryville would allow themselves — but even then only those who had children. The youngsters enjoyed the excitement and thrills of the various rides. While they were riding the Dragon's Tail, the parents would walk up and down the midway looking at the freaks. Standing before their canvas backdrops, the fat man and the bearded woman, the tattooed girl, the ape boy and many others caused the grey, look-alike citizens of Factoryville to stand in open-mouthed amazement. As the children grew up, they stopped enjoying the various rides of the amusement park and, like their parents, would stay at home and work

51

around the house on their days off.

But the freaks and all the other workers at the carnival continued to hold a special charm for one young man. He decided to join these "strangers" and worked at odd jobs around the park. The pay wasn't as good as it was at the funeral wreath factory, but it was fun to be around the roustabouts with their colorful tattoos and their wild stories. Most of all, he enjoyed being around the owner of the carnival, a man named J.P.T. Barnum who claimed to be the great-grandson of the famous P.T. of circus fame. One day as the young man was staring at one of the freaks, J.P.T., wearing his usual scarlet frock coat and tall, black silk hat, said: "Don't stare, son, it's not polite. We're all freaks, or at least we are supposed to be! Most people choose to be imitations, mere ciphers in a crowd. These delightful folk are being just who God made them to be . . . and you should do the same. The word 'freak,' my good lad, originally meant 'to be spontaneous,' to do something of 'sudden fancy.' It comes from an Old English word that means 'to dance.' Freaks are only people who dance, who are free of being what other people expect them to be. I know that freaks today are poor persons who are monstrosities — those of abnormal physical build or perhaps burnt-out hippies. But we are all intended to be playful and different: 'freaky.' " Besides being exposed to such a marvelous wisdom of life, the young man also learned to operate the roller coaster and the ferris wheel.

As the years passed, the oppressive silent power of the funeral wreath factory caused the number of paying customers to dwindle to almost nothing. The amusement park was going bankrupt! The workers and carnival folk began to drift away to various other carnivals and circuses. One day, J.P.T. Barnum, carrying a tattered suitcase, walked up to the young man, tossed him a set of keys and said, "Here are the keys to the main gate. Joyland is yours, my good man. I'm off to Baghdad!" For several years thereafter the carnival remained but a dusty ghost town, unused and unlighted. The young man did not return to work at the factory. Instead, he lived in a shack under the roller coaster and studied the books that J.P.T. left behind. In those silent and secluded years he changed greatly.

One evening, as a grey line of workers came down the hill — passing an identical grey line slowly moving up the hill toward the factory — a stranger appeared standing on a box beside the road. He wore a scarlet frock coat, and his voice rang out with the melody and authority of trumpets. "Friends," he said, "beware! You are becoming as lifeless as the plastic flowers you weave into empty circles. Do not be cowards . . . slaves of spiritlessness. If you trust only in the logical and secure, how can you ever dance, ever be alive? You must have faith. You must have faith in the fantastic — the truly fantastic. Without faith in the non-logical, you will be forever frozen in the narrow life of Factoryville. Come, be cured. Follow me, and we shall once again open the gates of Joyland. We all need some legitimate foolishness, or we will never taste the mystery of life. Come, it is time to play."

A few workers stopped and listened; others reflexively felt guilty and mechanically continued on toward home and their evening of work. To these he called out in a loud voice, "Friends, throw off your guilt. You feel guilty because of the unused, unlived life inside you. You are guilty because you are failing to become who you were intended to be. Do not be afraid to be different, to be *freaks*. Only those who fail to become who they were created to be are forced to find a cardboard security in a life's work

53

which is without meaning. Come, follow me to the hill." And a small group of them did just that. They dropped their tin lunch pails in a pile beside the road and climbed the hill toward the darkened amusement park.

Two nights later, in an explosion of brightly colored, twinkling lights and fluttering flags, the amusement park came alive. The enchanting music of a steam calliope filled the evening air. People came out onto their porches and looked toward the brightly lit hilltop. Many of them began to move in the direction of the resurrected carnival when from the great funeral wreath factory there came a shrill, banshee-like wail of a whistle. It was the signal to return to work — the sound that awakened deep, deep feelings of guilt.

The young man, seizing a megaphone, called out to the crowds that stood paralyzed by the work whistle. He said, "You all have a choice. There *are* real alternatives in life. Be brave . . . no, be foolish! Be foolish and . . . " Before he could finish, an earthquake shook the mountain as if it were a dust rag. Houses trembled, and one of the tall, black smokestacks on the funeral wreath factory collapsed in a giant mushroom cloud of grey soot. From cracks that jigsawed across the top of the mountain, white clouds of steam jetted skyward. Then with a tremendous roar, as if ten thousand cannons had been fired at once, the entire top of the mountain blew off. Streams of fire, showers of rocks and sprays of steam and dust shot thousands of feet skyward. The fiery dust turned the moon red as a fountain of flaming sparks fell over all of Factoryville. Spilling over the rim of the jagged top of the mountain came a scarlet-yellow river of fire cascading downward, then another river and yet another. These luminous fiery rivers were flowing directly toward Factoryville. Panic seized the population as people scurried off their front porches. Which way should they flee? The only safe ground was that of the two hills. As the numerous rivers joined into a single, mighty onrush of liquid fire, the people fled in two directions. Many found refuge in the upper stories of the fortress-like factory while others poured through the open gates of the amusement park.

The river of fire that swept through the city completely destroyed it — and it would be years before the earth had cooled enough for anyone to even attempt to walk across the no-man's-land between the amusement park and the factory. And so, the refugees of Factoryville became the residents of whichever place they had sought out for "temporary" safety. The ones who worked and lived in the funeral wreath factory called those who found refuge in Joyland "freaks" because they were so different from all the "normal" people. And those who lived and played in Joyland never went to confession or worked overtime.

Every year on the anniversary of the mountain's volcanic eruption, the people of Joyland celebrated. They threw fireballs into the air and launched rockets that exploded into millions of stars, rejoicing that the fire which came from the mountain was not one of destruction or punishment but was rather the flame of freedom and life.

This story which I have related is, so I am told by persons of high reputation, a tale of how fireworks came to be. And so, today, whenever you see a sky-rocket or Roman candle decorating the night sky with fire, it should remind you to ask yourself, "Where have I chosen to live: in Joyland . . . or in a funeral wreath factory?"

ÄLAK ÎUGABÆ GUARDIAN ANGEL... THERE ARE SOME WHO HAVE MANY EYES... THERE ARE SOME WHO ARE ONLY EYES~

Of THE SUN

And SOME WHO ARE All BURST OF LIGHT~

BRIGHTER THAN THE LIGHT

The Fig Tree

For several years the young fig tree had been without fruit. She had drunk fully of the rain, soaked up the warm rays of the sun, and absorbed her share of goodness from the earth, but yet no fruit had been found on her branches. The owner of the orchard had no patience for what he considered parasites. "Cut her down!" he ordered the gardener.

"Please, sir," said the gardener, "please give her just one more year. Allow me to nurture her and to challenge her. One more year, and then if she is still barren, well . . . I will have her cut down."

Shaking his head and mumbling to himself, the owner agreed as he walked away from the gardener saying, "One more year, but that's all — one more year."

The gardener began by putting manure around the tree. The fig tree pretended not to notice and only raised her head higher in the sky. He then dug about the tree with his shovel, and as he did he spoke to the tree, "Everyone and everything that lives has a vocation. It's the calling to be yourself."

The fig tree said nothing but only sighed inwardly. "Who wants to be themselves if they're only a fig tree!" she thought to herself. The fig tree, you see, thought that fig trees were too common. She had tried to be an apple tree for years, but no apples appeared on her branches. She even went to college and took all the courses necessary to become a pear tree, but no pears appeared. So she then resorted to taking a home correspondence course entitled, "How to be a Banana Tree." From this and all her other efforts

57

only frustration and the fruits of failure grew on her.

"I need to find a job that I can enjoy," said the fig tree.

"A job and a vocation," replied the gardener, "are two very different things, my dear fig tree. A vocation has about it a sense of mystery, but a job is like a task — it is something to be done and not lived! A vocation comes from your very roots — from deep down in the dark depths of yourself. And you have Fig Tree roots."

"No thanks," said the fig tree, "I prefer to be more novel. I think I'll go over to the laboratory and have them 'cross-gene' me; you know, have them perform a graft with some other tree so that I can be really special. Who knows, perhaps I can become a 'banapple tree.' Think of the news coverage, not to mention the demand for my fruit, if they could shake up my genes like that."

The gardener shook his head and stopped digging as he said, "There is something most special about you even now, little tree. You can be creative in the truest way by living out the mystery of your 'fig-treeness.' You then become not only something special but also something sacred! By responding to the challenge to become yourself you will find yourself in the presence of the real mystery — God. However, both life and God will escape you if you attempt to be what you are not intended to be. And remember, you only have one more year — for the master said he was going to have you chopped down if you do not bear fruit this year."

"I wish I could run away," said the fig tree. "Oh, to have the gift of locomotion like dogs and cats. There's an idea: I could become a traveling tree. I would need special roots that could stand the wear and tear of walking and still be able to sink deep into the soil when it is dinner time. But where would I

58

go to learn such a trick?"

"No, fig tree," interrupted the gardener, "forget about being novel — about being a 'one and only' kind of tree — and be creative. I know ... I know for sure that if you would only listen to what's in your roots you would be the most special, the most creative and lovely tree in all the world."

"Listen to my roots?" asked the fig tree. "What's down there?"

"Your dreams are there," said the gardener, "and your history, your passions and desires and other dark mysteries."

"Such as?" asked the fig tree.

"Such as the memories of who you were even before you were a fig tree. In each of us are memories of all the different stages of growth over billions of years. When we begin to pay attention — to hear them, feel them, sense them — their touch guides us to become fully who we are," answered the gardener.

"That's very interesting, but how can anyone think with such a horrible smell everywhere?" asked the fig tree, holding her head as high in the sky as possible.

"I have surrounded you with manure. I realize that it's not the most pleasant of perfumes, but it is one of the 'real' smells of life. Your life, mine — everyone's — has its share of crap. We all prefer to get rid of it as soon as possible. But we have to learn to live with it if we wish to grow. You, like all of us, must be willing to live with the manure of defeat, mistakes, failures, sickness, pain, suffering and even sin. These are the fertilizers of life. They are really the stuff that enables you to grow, to get in touch with strengths you never knew you had. Yes, my young friend, manure is an essential companion for those who wish to be fully mature."

The fig tree was silent. What could she say — the

gardener was so philosophical. But even if she didn't have a quick reply, she didn't believe that all her pain and frustration had helped her to grow to be anything but a failure!

The gardener then took a paperback book from his hip pocket and said, "Listen to these lines from my favorite poet, E. E. Cummings: 'To be nobody but yourself in a world which is doing its best, day and night, to make you everybody else, means to fight the hardest battle which any human being can fight, and never stop fighting.' You are not a human being, my dear fig tree, but it doesn't make any difference; the truth remains."

"That's what I've been doing all these years," said the fig tree. "I've been fighting not to be 'everybody.' I want to be *special*."

"But," answered the gardener, "that doesn't mean becoming a hybrid or having some graft done; it means being *'nobody but yourself.'* The source of what you desire is to be honest to your roots — honest regardless of the struggle."

Not a sound could be heard in the orchard except the dry summer wind rustling the leaves of the olive trees. Both the gardener and the fig tree were silent for a long time. The fig tree was thinking. She was thinking clearly for the first time in years. "Yes," she said to herself, "it was right for me to fight; only I guess . . . I guess I was fighting for the wrong thing. In trying to be free of what everybody else wanted me to be, I tried to make myself into something that was unique. I was trying to be novel instead of creative. That was my problem; I see it clearly now. Why not pour all my energy into letting whatever is down there in my roots flow upward, let it bloom on my branches and mature into ripe fruit?"

The sun was riding low in the western sky as the gardener picked up his tools and prepared to go home. Once again he approached the fig tree, and with a smile on his lips he asked her, "Well, my friend?"

Taking a deep breath, she rose to the fullness of her height and said in a voice loud enough for all the trees in the orchard to hear, "I think I'll be a Fig Tree!"

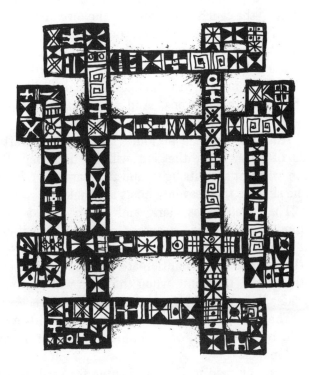

Falling Stars

The other night I had a most unusual and compelling dream. The setting of my dream was quite commonplace; there were three people seated in easy chairs and engaged in conversation. What made the dream so extraordinary was the identity of the three: Daniel, the prophet, Jesus of Nazareth and Barbara Cronkite, the anchorwoman on the evening news! The action began with Daniel, the prophet, speaking: "It shall be a time unsurpassed in distress . . . many of those who sleep in the dust of the earth shall awake . . . but the wise shall shine brightly like the splendor of the heavens. And those who lead the many to justice shall be like the stars forever."

"And during that period," added Jesus, "after trials of every sort, the sun will be darkened, the moon will not shed its light, and the stars will fall out of the skies as the heavenly hosts are shaken."

"That sounds as dark and foreboding as the evening news," replied Barbara Cronkite, "or is it just that season again? The coming of winter and the end of the year makes us anticipate the apocalyptic end of the world, that time when the stars will fall from the skies."

"The fact that the stars will fall," returned Jesus, "could be a bad sign, or it could be a beautiful sign; it all depends."

"Yes," chimed in Daniel, leaning forward toward the other two, "there is an ancient story, told around the evening fires, that stars fall from the skies only at appointed times. They fall from the heavens gently, as do the brilliant autumn leaves. And, luminous, they descend whirling upon the winds of outer space."

"Ah, yes, Daniel," agreed Jesus. "I often heard that story as a child. The Lord God, blessed be his name, when it is autumn in heaven, shakes the giant tree of paradise and millions of brilliant leaves fall to earth. They float lazily downward. Then, as they approach this planet they become impatient and anxious to reach the earth, so they shoot toward their destination, sparkling with eagerness and eternal energy."

"Then shooting stars," inquired Barbara, "are really luminous leaves falling from the giant tree of paradise?"

"That's correct, Barbara," replied Daniel. "As Jesus said, 'the heavenly hosts will be shaken,' but such a disturbance in the heavens is not a cause for alarm but rather a cause for joy!"

"And I might add," offered Jesus, "that every shooting star you see racing across the night sky has as its destination an open and loving womb. You and I — all of us — are only leaves from that giant tree of heaven. We are, Barbara, divine energy, starlight fused with flesh."

Smiling, Barbara said, "If that theory is indeed correct, it may explain why we all secretly dream of being stars. We simply dream of becoming what we truly are! It would also explain why we are attracted to personalities who are 'stars' in sports, films and entertainment, for energy attracts energy. We are magnetically drawn toward those whose light radiates outward with a minimum of obstruction. Perhaps it is a law of the cosmos that energy is attracted to energy." After a moment of silence she continued, "Then it follows that the star of Bethlehem was just another luminous leaf falling from the great tree of paradise, that its energy entered the womb of a wait-

63

ing Mary. And if so, you, Jesus, or you, Daniel, are but stars who fell to earth?"

"That's right," responded Daniel, "and, Barbara, you too are a star — not simply on television, but long before that. And that stardom belongs to everyone. But once the energy of a star fuses with flesh, the memory of what it is and where it came from can easily be forgotten. Countless stars sleep in the dust of their earthen bodies. But once they are awakened they begin to shine like a candle raging quiet in the night, just as shooting stars are silent in their splendor."

"But how does the former splendor ever shine out through the flesh?" asked Barbara.

In response to that question Jesus said, "If you pour out your bread for the hungry, if you bind up the wounds of the soul, then will your true light shine for all to see."

"If!" exclaimed Barbara. "*If* is a word of tremendous influence, even *if* it is only two letters long."

"Well said, Barbara!" beamed Jesus. "If you bind up the wounds of the soul, if . . . if . . . Indeed, if you have faith the size of a mustard seed . . . If you take time to practice, you will become a great musician. If your heart is filled with love, you will do all things well. If you can swallow a tongue swollen with the desire to say, 'I told you so!' If you can forgive seven times seventy times — if, if, if . . . "

"Strange," added Daniel after a reflective pause, "that such a small word as *if* has the power to prevent the light from raging quiet in the night, from shining like a city seated on a hill for all to see."

"I remember a story about an old holy man and his disciple," returned Jesus. "One night a young seeker came to the hermitage of this holy man and said to him, 'Abba, I wish to be holy. I have read all the sacred scriptures. I have fasted for years, have

64

trained my body to be totally obedient. I have prayed the long night vigils and have spent forty days in absolute solitude in the most remote area of the desert. Please, Abba, what else should I do?' The old man stood up tall and erect. He raised his arms above his head, his fingers flickering like luminous lamps, and he said softly, 'Well, my son, you could become fire!' "

Barbara, Daniel and Jesus sat for a long time in silence. Then Daniel spoke, "But 'to become fire' you must first move beyond all the *ifs* of life. True wisdom is to know who you are, to know you are light. Those who know and who have removed all the ifs shine brightly like the stars of the night sky. Having removed the ifs they find time to study, to practice, to play with their children, to help the poor . . . time to pray, to go deep — deep inside themselves — and to touch that luminous leaf shimmering at the center of their hearts. Not *if* they had time, they *have* time. Not *if* they could be kind; because they want passionately to be kind, they indeed become kind. Truly, this age is unsurpassed in distress, and daily the darkness grows because in so many of our lives there are too many ifs."

"Each night," replied Barbara, "from Monday through Friday, I report the news, and I can assure both of you that the world is living on the edge of darkness. We desperately need a Buddha at the U.N. or a Lao Tzu advising the leaders of China. Israel — and all the world — needs another Moses. And, Jesus, are there not other carpenters who can find that luminous leaf in their hearts? Ah, the darkness today is strong: war, greed, the starvation of millions, a lack of reverence for life, and so much sickness of the heart — if only God would send us another savior like you, Jesus. It seems that it has been far too long since it has been autumn-time in heaven, far too long since

65

our earth was illuminated by such a star as a Joan of Arc, Chang Tzu, Isaiah or Jesus."

"But, Barbara, all is not darkness," said Jesus. "When I look out at the world, I do see the splendor of light. There is an old rabbi in Warsaw, for example, whose face shines like the sun each time he prays from the Torah, and a Sufi master, a dervish in Istanbul, who is radiant as he whirls in sacred dance. And down on the Tennessee River I know a weatherworn, white frame Baptist church where each time the black pastor preaches of God's great love, his face takes on all the luminous brilliance of the planet Venus . . . . "

At this point Daniel interrupted Jesus, saying, "Yes, Barbara, all is not darkness. I know of a truck driver on a busy schedule who stopped to help someone fix a flat on a deserted highway. And there's a married couple in Detroit who have rejected the easy-out of divorce and are struggling to resolve their problems, but only with great personal effort and suffering. Or that woman in Denver who takes time each week to visit her lonely neighbor and . . . well, we could go on and on, but these *are* times when the light has broken loose from the flesh and *does* shine marvelously for all to see."

"Yes, I'm sure that all these examples are true," replied Barbara, "but if you look at the news of the world each night, as I do; if you look at what is happening not simply in your own neighborhood but across the entire earth, what you will see is treachery, violence, exploitation, faithlessness, greed and uncontrolled hatred. No, my holy friends, I grant that there may be moments of flickering light and that there may be star-like sacred energy within us, but it is buried so deeply in the dust of our flesh that we would need another savior to bring it forth at this time! No, not a savior; we need a multitude of

66

messiahs if . . . if the darkness is not to cover us all."

Now at that very moment the discussion was interrupted by the appearance before me of a tall and beautiful angel. The angel's wings opened and closed silently, revealing a rainbow of luminous colors. The angel raised one hand, a long index finger pointing skyward, and said, "Do not be afraid. I have been sent to announce to you good news. In heaven, once again, it is autumn. The giant tree of paradise is scarlet with sacred leaves, and God is shaking the tree. Fear not; watch the night skies for shooting stars. Awake! Remember who you are! Remember, for it has been autumn in heaven now for sixty, seventy or perhaps even ninety years! The time is ripe . . . . "

At that moment the dream suddenly vanished, frightened away by the bells of my alarm clock. But the vision of the luminous leaf still pulses in my heart.

The Soul Dream

Once upon a time, outside God's office in heaven, a long line of new, unused souls stretched as far as the eye could see, waiting to be given their life's assignments. The two souls closest to the office door were chatting about what they wanted to be.

"I am going to ask if I can be a black person," said the soul who was second in line.

"Oh, really! Why?" asked the one who stood in front.

"Well, for one thing, black is my favorite color," replied the other soul, "and from what I have seen down on earth, black people seem to enjoy life more than those of other colors. And you, since you're next in line, what are you going to ask to become?"

The soul standing next to the office door replied, "I'm going to ask God if I can be a home. Ever since I can remember, I have dreamed of being a beautiful home — a house with a good, strong foundation and a basement, a big front porch, a large yard with trees all around me and . . . . "

At that moment the door to God's office opened, and an angel appeared to announce, with a drill-sergeant's voice, "Next!" The soul who wanted to be a house entered and stood with reverence at the side of God's great roll-top desk. The great, old oak desk was piled high with papers, folders, stacks and stacks of request slips and a large unfolded map of the universe. "Yes, my beautiful young soul," said God in a gentle voice, "and what would you like to be? As a good administrator I always try to let my souls choose what they want to be. They're happier that way, and the cosmos is more efficient. Naturally, dear," and here God smiled more kindly at her, "sometimes we have an emergency, and I must ask a soul to put aside personal desires for the greater good of the universe. But you, dear, what would you like to become — a bird or beast, a human, a mountain?"

"Lord God, Beloved One," said the soul, "after much thought and reflection, I would like to become a home." Then she bowed, beaming with eager anticipation.

"So let it be done as you desire and I decree," said the Lord God as he rang a golden desk-top bell, the kind that used to sit on hotel reservation counters. Instantly, an angel appeared, wiping crumbs from his beard, apparently having been interrupted in the middle of his lunch. The angel stood at attention as God looked closely at his large map of the universe. Tapping his finger on the area representing the planet Earth, right at the center of America, God said, "Take this lovely soul down to Akron, Ohio, where she shall become a brand new home — for with God all things are possible." At once the angel picked up the soul in his strong arms and like a flash of lightning streaked down toward Earth.

"There," said the angel as he set her gently on the ground, "your heart's desire is now a reality. God's will be done." But something was amiss, for the soul felt ill-at-ease. The house that the soul was now wedded to for all eternity didn't seem to fit right, and there was a cold draught blowing underneath her. She felt odd and uncomfortable; it was nothing at all like she thought being a home would feel. "Do you have a mirror on you?" she asked the angel. "I need to look at myself. This home doesn't seem to fit at all." The angel produced a mirror from inside a pocket under one of his wings and held it up so that the soul could see herself.

A sharp, painful cry of shock was the soul's response. "What am I? What did God do to me? I'm not a home, I'm a trailer! Look, instead of a basement I have two sets of tandem wheels under me. No wonder I feel chilly breezes and feel so naked; my gas and water pipes are all exposed. And look at my dimensions — I'm only fourteen feet wide but all of seventy feet long — oh my!" And feeling her sides she moaned, "I'm aluminum and tin, not brick, stone or wood. Oh, angel, go back and tell God that he's made a mistake! I want to return to heaven at once and have this error corrected." As the angel sped away heavenward, she slumped over, weeping great tears.

In the midst of her crying, gentle hands began to stroke her, and quiet, kind words attempted to ease her sorrow. Raising her head she noticed for the first time that she was surrounded by many other trailers. Still sobbing, she asked, "Where am I?"

A long trailer, with imitation wooden siding, parked next to her said, "Deary, you're in the Akron Acme Sales display lot. We're all brand new, just like you. We're waiting for someone to buy us and take us away. Why are you so sad, dear; why all the tears?"

"Oh, there's been a terrible mistake," she cried, "some divine clerical error or something. I asked God to become a home, not a trailer! Look at me! This is not at all what I wanted to be in life."

When she said this, some of the trailers who had at first been concerned about her turned away saying, "Who does she think she is anyway? What's so terrible about being a trailer; what's the matter with the way we look?" The trailer with the imitation wooden siding, however, continued to try to comfort her. "Deary, you have to be brave; it's God's will. You must simply accept it — 'que, sera, sera,' what will be, will be."

70

"I will not accept it!" she snapped back. "I've already filed a complaint. God himself said that all things are possible with him. I will *insist* that this mistake be corrected. I want to be a beautiful home and not some cheap, tinny trailer!"

Now, while the day had been calm, clear and cloudless, suddenly the wind began blowing in strong, violent gusts. Dust and leaves swirled around in great, brown clouds, as the trailers looked at one another with anxious glances. Their greatest fear was realized when the civil defense tornado sirens began to wail. As the tornado swept down upon the Akron Acme Sales lot with full force, each of the trailers hugged the ground and prayed. At the center of the tornado was a circle of static stillness, and at the center of that circle was the dissatisfied trailer. Out of the eerie, death-like silence came a very firm voice, "I Am Who Am and I do not make mistakes! Now stop this childish crying and straighten up. You asked to be a home and I made you one; you are not a trailer, you are a *mobile home*. There is no way now to become the soul of anything else. I am a creative and original God; I never recycle souls. I also do not make clerical errors."

"Please, oh please, Lord God," she begged, "make an exception for me. What am I to do? My dream is a disaster! Please, God, change me; please work a miracle. With you all things are possible; you said so yourself."

"I'm sorry, poor little soul, that you're unhappy being what I made you, but what is, IS!" said God sadly. "And if you want your dream to come true, you'll just have to be creative." And with the roar of ten thousand thunderstorms the tornado swept upward and vanished. As the dust settled and calm returned to the Akron Acme Sales lot, it appeared that a miracle had happened. Not a single mobile home was destroyed — or even slightly damaged. There was great rejoicing among all of them — except one. That night, she cried herself to sleep.

The next ten years passed slowly and painfully. First, she was sold to a family who used her only while they built a new home. They parked her on the building site, and it was a distressing experience for her to watch a "real" house slowly take shape as she tasted the impossibility of her own dream. Each night as she went to sleep she prayed, "God, help me to accept your holy will." And each morning when she awoke and saw herself, she hated what she saw. After two years she was sold to a construction worker who never cleaned her or cared for her needs. She was only a place for him to sleep or throw his wild beer parties. For three years she belonged to him, and then, dirty and abused, she was passed on to a divorcee with three small children. The mobile home enjoyed having children around her, but they did a lot of damage that was never repaired. The woman who now owned her was on welfare and lacked the money or desire to keep her clean. Four years later — battered, paint peeling, windows cracked, marred and neglected — she became the home of a young married couple with a small infant. They towed her to Omaha, Nebraska, where she was parked with a hundred other look-alikes in a large trailer court called Sunset Estates. Like so many other young married couples, they were poor and struggling, and the mobile home was all they could afford. But, unlike her previous owners, the young couple took pride in their home, even if it was only a fourteen-by-seventy foot trailer. They cleaned and swept, painted and repaired her. Slowly she began to feel valued and loved. Each night after all was quiet, she would pray, "Lord, I do try to accept your will that I am who I am. Help me to live out that mystery." And each night she

72

would fall asleep dreaming her ageless dream of being a beautiful home on a solid foundation with tall trees and a long, lazy, green lawn around her.

Within a few years the young couple was able to put some money into savings, which pleased them but only worried the mobile home. She thought to herself, "When they have enough money, they will sell me and buy or build a permanent home. Then what will happen to me?" Now one night as she was praying before falling asleep, for some reason she recalled the last words God had spoken when he appeared as a tornado. God had said, "If you want your dream to come true, you must be creative." Perhaps it was her anger at God for making her a trailer, even though he did call her a mobile home, or her disappointment, or her being lost in self-pity, but she had not in all the ten years reflected on that bit of divine advice. " . . . be creative?" she thought to herself, "What did God mean by that?" And she also recalled another statement, "I Am Who Am and I don't make mistakes!" As she was turning these thoughts over in her mind, she heard the young couple talking quietly in their bedroom as they lay together. They were dreaming about their future home surrounded by tall trees with a beautiful lawn. As they fell asleep together, lost in their common dream, the mobile home had a brilliant idea. All the next day she was so busy with her planning that she forgot to pray her daily prayer to accept God's will.

That very night, when the couple was asleep, she focused all her spiritual energy around their bed. Then she began to chant softly over and over, "Let's move out of the city onto a little piece of land, and then after a few years we could build a home." All night long for three nights in a row, she surrounded them with her energy, chanting that single sentence. On the morning after the third night the husband said, "Maggie . . . let's move out of the city onto a little piece of land, and then after a few years we could build a home." And so it happened. With the help of a bank loan they purchased a quiet little ten-acre site in the country — not too far from the city — with tall trees and plenty of green grass. They moved their mobile home onto their new land, and, although they were pleased with their new lifestyle, they began to put away some of the money left after their monthly land payments in order to build their future dream house. After a couple of years the mobile home began to put phase two of her plan into action. Each night as the couple slept, she chanted over and over, "We'll never save enough money to build a new house. Why don't we convert this trailer into our permanent home?" This time it took longer than three nights. But one morning, after she had been working all night long for nearly three months, she was delighted to hear the wife say, "Mike . . . you know, we'll never save enough money to build a new house. Why don't we convert this trailer into our permanent home?" And so they did.

First they built a strong foundation of concrete blocks underneath her. Then they tore off part of an outside wall on one side and built a small extension. Later they did the same on the other side. All this cutting and ripping of her sides was painful for the mobile home, but she bore the pain like a mother giving birth to a child. No longer did she have a fourteen-by-seventy figure, but she was beginning to look like a "real" house. Next they added a pitched roof; they placed real cedar wood on her sides, added a grand screened-in porch and a stone fireplace. With tall, stately maple trees surrounding her and children playing about her on the lawn, her heart was full to overflowing — especially when the family called her the most beautiful name in all the world: "home."

74

One night when she, together with all the family, was deep in sleep, God came to pay a visit. Only this time the Lord did not come as a tornado but rather as a quiet, gentle night breeze. She awoke at once and bowed deeply. "Lord God," she said, "who am I that you should come to me? Behold, I am your hand-maid. Be it done to me as you say."

"Hi," said God, "I like the way you talk; it's got a nice ring to it. I was in the neighborhood and thought I would stop by to see how things were going."

"Oh, thank you, Lord God," she returned, "I'm fine. In fact, I've never been happier in all my life. I am now what I have always wanted to be; I am a home — a *real* home. But I must confess, I thought for the longest time that it would never ever happen."

"Good . . . good. I'm glad that you're happy," said God as he strolled off into the evening. "It's like I always say, 'with God, all things are possible.'"

The Alien

Long, long ago, there lived a very large family. It was, in fact, the largest family in the world! It was so large that the parents did not even know the exact number of their children. But although it was of such great size, it was still a loving family. All the brothers and sisters possessed a wonderful sense of family unity, and they joyfully shared the great house in which they all lived. This home was as beautiful as the family that filled its many, many rooms.

Now, while the children were so numerous that they were beyond counting, their parents loved each of them with a personal love. And since the greatest love that any parent can give to a child is the gift of freedom, these children all had the freedom to be truly themselves. As a result, while they had all come from the same parents, they did not look or act alike. Some wore rich and luxurious furs, others delightfully dressed all in feathers, and still others wore suits of soft bark and long flowing capes of scarlet leaves. Yet in spite of all their variety and many differences, they lived united in love and harmony with each other.

One day the father of the family came to the top of the staircase at the center of the great house and called all his children together. His long white hair flowed gracefully over his shoulders, and his beard cascaded down his chest like Niagara Falls in the winter. Facing the whole family he announced with great glee: "After so many years during which our house has been without a baby, we announce with great joy that you have a little baby brother!"

All the children cheered loudly, for indeed it had been a very long time since a baby had been born to the family. The family all gathered around eager to see the newest arrival, who, while not looking at all like any of the others, was greeted with songs and rejoicing.

The brothers and sisters lovingly took turns caring for the infant. However, as he became older something very disturbing became apparent. While he seemed bright and could do many things, he had an emotional block — an island of insanity — for he believed that he was an alien!

Yes, the child believed that he did not belong to his own family. He was convinced that he had been left on their doorstep and really belonged to someone else. The family house was not his home, these were not his brothers and sisters but were strangers, strangers who were his potential enemies. As he grew older the problem also grew. He refused to speak the common language and instead made up one of his own, one which the others could not understand. This only confirmed to him that he was an alien. Next he began building a wall to separate himself from the others. He built a small, wooden playhouse-box in his room and called it "home."

He frequently stole from his brothers and sisters and treated them cruelly. On occasion he would leave his playhouse-box and take little trips around the rest of the house. When he did so, he would carry with him a small canvas copy of his box, and if he stayed overnight somewhere other than in his own room, he would pitch his little canvas box and sleep in it. But wherever he went, he always left litter behind him. He was a careless, messy, self-centered child.

Finally, his brothers and sisters went to their father to complain and demand that something be done about their barbarian brother. "He's cruel and thinks it fun to hurt us," said one sister. "He took my fur coat and left me with none," added a brother. "Father," chimed in another, "you should never have given him that chemistry set for his birthday. He fills the house with smoke and the whole place stinks. He's getting worse, and we think that he should be put in an institution before he does any more damage."

The kindly father held up his hand for quiet, as many other children began to voice their complaints. "Yes, yes, I know, and I am sorry for all the pain that each of you has felt because of him. But we must be patient; your little brother is emotionally ill, and we must not treat him too harshly."

But as time passed, the child's behavior continued to grow worse. Daily, the child would claim more and more of the great house as his own, driving the others away with threats or with vicious attacks. His brothers and sisters would have loved to discipline him themselves, but their father had urged them to be patient.

One day the father once again called the entire family together to make an announcement. "We have decided after much thought that, even though we are old and already have a great family, we shall have another baby. It is our hope that what our sick and disturbed boy needs is a companion."

This time no great cheer went up from the rest of the family. They thought to themselves, "One spoiled baby in the family is enough. What will it be like to have two of them in the same house?"

The kindly and loving father could easily read their thoughts and replied, "Children, children — my son, the cedar; and you, my beautiful daughter, dolphin; and you, noble deer, and all the rest of you — I know that you have suffered much at the hands of our disturbed child, but this new child will be differ-

78

ent. We have poured all our love, all our dreams and hopes, into him. This child will be different; he will heal his disturbed brother and make him well. Please wait and see."

From the moment of his birth the family could see that their new baby brother was indeed different. As his brothers and sisters clustered around his crib, he smiled and spoke to them in the common tongue. He reached out to each of them with affection and trust. Great joy filled the large house, for indeed their father seemed to be right — perhaps this new child could help their disturbed brother.

The new child grew in wisdom and age — his teachers were his brothers and sisters, the trees and lakes, lilies and wheat, each of whom taught him much. His brother, the son who thought of himself as an outsider, at first rejoiced in the arrival of his brother, but as soon as it became apparent that his baby brother did not also consider himself to be an alien, a stranger to the others who lived in the great house, he grew suspicious and began teasing him. As they grew a little older, however, the disturbed boy secretly longed to believe that what his brother kept telling him was true, that he was not an alien — that this was really home to both of them, this vast and wondrous place where they lived. Living as an alien and a stranger was lonely, but at the same time, thought the older brother, was it not his fate in living the life of an alien to be lonely and isolated in the midst of hostile enemies? "Yes," he resolved, "walls are my only defense, and I must build bigger and bigger ones."

As he was extending the height of the walls around his playhouse, his younger brother spoke to him about how important it was that he stop this madness. "Your chances of surviving, brother," said the younger boy, "are like a snowball in summer.

You will die from all the poison that you are creating with your little chemistry set. And worse yet, your own hate will destroy you. You must learn to love all those you call your enemies: your sister bird and brother fish, your brother ant and sister spider — even your brother snake whom you love to kill on sight. You must learn to have a love affair with all those who share this great house. We all have the same father — you and I, and all the rest who live here. It is vital that we care for one another."

The older brother cursed loudly and threw his hammer at his little brother. "Shut up; you're the crazy one, not me." But his little brother continued, "Brother, we have only one choice: either love or perish. If you do not love all, you will destroy yourself as well as our beautiful house. The very walls you are building to defend yourself will destroy you." Unable to listen to these words any longer, the older brother jumped down from his wall and threw the younger boy to the floor. In his attempt to silence him, the violence of his anger was so great that he killed his little brother.

Seeing his brother dead, a victim of his hate, he knew that what he had done was wrong, and for the first time he felt real guilt. He begged his father to forgive him — which the father did, with great love and compassion.

Thereafter, the older brother often quoted the words of his little brother. He even attempted to live in the way he had been encouraged to live — in a life-style of harmony and deep love for all with whom he shared the great house. Each year he celebrated the birthday of his brother whom he had killed. And each year he grew to feel more and more a member of the family and less and less a stranger, an outsider in his own home. He called the celebration of his brother's birthday "the feast that I am not an alien." And each year he improved and came closer to full mental and emotional and spiritual health. With each festival he became more and more sane.

The old and kindly father would smile, his great, white beard cascading down his chest, and would say, "Soon, children, your little brother will be perfectly well and whole. Soon he will truly be one of the family."

The Mirror Of God

In the beginning, the very beginning, there was only God. Actually, there was no beginning — at least as we understand a beginning. God simply was, and God was all there was. Because of this God could not see what he looked like. Creation had not happened yet, and so there were no mirrors in which God might see his image. As a result God brushed his teeth, washed his face, and combed his beautiful long beard without the aid of a looking glass.

"I wonder what I look like," God often thought. This itch to see his image came and went as do all the haunting thoughts of life (although since there was as yet no such thing as time, we cannot say how long God reflected on this problem). Finally God decided to create something in which he might see his reflection. First God created light, which would be necessary for his reflection to become visible. Then God created a looking glass and called it "creation." God looked into his new invention and exclaimed, "Hmmm, beautiful!" And so, God knew that he was beautiful, good and wholesome. Each day this cosmic mirror reflected back to God the infinite variety of his beauty. Each morning, as God brushed his teeth and looked into his mirror, he took delight in what he saw. Each night before retiring he looked into the darkness of the night-mirror and found pleasure in the image of his dark side.

For millions upon millions of years God found much joy at seeing his reflection in the mirror of creation. But, while being pleased, something was missing, for this mirror showed only a part of the Divine

Image. Gradually another haunting thought began to surface in the mind of God: "Is it possible to create a mirror so special that it might reflect what is present in my heart?" Another hundred million years went by as quickly as the movement of a humming-bird's wings, until one day God actually decided to create such a marvelous mirror. And so God created man and woman, the first of the earthpeople. God was excited to see the reflection of his heart in them as the two made love, showed compassion for one another and forgave each other's daily failings. "In-deed," thought God, "this has to be my finest crea-tion." Each time he gazed into the double mirror of man and woman he would exclaim, "Hmmmmm, so beautiful!"

Now these first earthpeople had no mirrors in which they might see themselves, aside from each other's eyes. They did have the giant looking glass of creation in which they could see part of their re-flection. However both these mirrors reflected only that which is good and beautiful. One hot day, after they had finished their lunch and were resting in the cool shade of a tall tree, a strange thing happened. Slinking into the garden came a large serpent, colored green with shades of violet and blue markings. The creature had such a handsome face that they could not take their eyes off him. At his left side the serpent carried a gift — a round looking glass in a smooth wooden frame with a carved handle — which he held up for the man and woman to gaze upon. Looking into the mirror they saw, for the first time, the "other side" of themselves. In the serpent's mirror they saw reflected the deep-hearted desire to be more than a reflection of God. Glittering before their eyes was the desire to *be* God, filled with all power and authority. Fearful of what they saw in the serpent's gift, they quickly turned away, denying that such an image had ever been there. But the beautiful creature spoke again with words dipped in honey and gently persuaded them to look again . . . and again. Man and woman became spellbound by what they saw, and the serpent convinced them to put their heart's desire into action — to take steps necessary to become gods. And so they did.

That evening in paradise, at sunset, as the birds were ending their daysong and the night stars were appearing in the west, God decided to look into his special mirror. But now he no longer saw that which is good and beautiful. Instead God saw sin smudged upon his image as he looked into the mirror of man and woman. He placed his hand first to his face, then to his heart, and after doing so realized that the smudge was not upon his heart but upon his mirror. Compared with the sunset mirror of creation, the double looking glass of his earthchildren appeared as some funhouse mirror, twisting and distorting the glorious beauty of his image. Distressed, God banished his prized two-fold mirror from his sight, and as he closed the gates to paradise he leaned back against a great palm tree, cupped his face in his hands, and wept with all his heart. All that night the entire mirror of God's creation wept with him.

During the centuries that followed God frequently wept floods of tears, since each time he looked into his double mirror it had become even more distorted and smudged. He would vow never to look again . . . then he would relent and once more turn his eye to his mirror. He saw goodness and beauty, but there was also much that was ugly and out of focus.

Centuries flowed into centuries until one day God had a glowing idea. Leaning way out over the railing on the porch of heaven, God stooped down to earth and whispered into the ear of a special earthchild.

84

Leaning back again, God sat on his front porch the remainder of the day and well into the evening, rocking slowly in his great rocking chair and smiling from ear to ear.

The earthchild grew into a man and did all the things that earthpeople do. Yet, while being so much the same as his fellow earthpeople, he was at the same time very different. One thing that made him different was the echo. Ever since he had been a child, the echo sounded in his heart. Sometimes it was faint; at other times it was louder, and at still other times it was not there at all. Finally, one day, he felt prompted to speak of the echo to his family and to the others in his village. His mother smiled and was not surprised; mothers tend to believe that anything is possible for their sons. His father was a wise man, and he knew human nature. He began to worry about the consequences of what his son had told him. His aunts and uncles were another matter. At first shocked and then filled with indignation, they responded, "Anyone who hears echoes is crazy in the head!" The young man wondered if perhaps they were right — perhaps he was mad.

His favorite cousin was renowned in that district for his special insight, and so, desiring to know the truth, he went to see him. He asked, "Do you sense anything different about me?" And his cousin, who at the moment happened to be in the midst of a crowd of people, replied, "Cousin, from the beginning both of us have been different. I, even as a child, heard a strange voice within me, and so I am where I am. And I sense that in you such a voice also is echoing. But, cousin, beware, for the multitudes are upset by that which is different." And so the young man left to ponder on the mystery of the echo.

Among the earthpeople there was a great taboo. It was forbidden to see one's own image in a pool of water or in a looking glass — at the cost of losing one's soul. Perhaps the taboo was some aged relic left from the garden days of the primal parents. Perhaps it was the result of the belief that the soul was but a reflection, and that by stopping to reflect on the reflection one would be held prisoner in the looking glass. Of course the greater the taboo, the greater the desire — and earthpeople had a great desire to gaze upon their images. And so it is not surprising that the strictest injunction was placed upon spending more time in front of a mirror than was absolutely necessary to straighten a tie or comb one's hair.

As a result, a very private ritual developed among earthpeople. This ritual, which was so ancient that no one could remember when or where it began, was performed only when one was totally alone. The person would stand before a mirror, looking deeply into its magic surface, and would say (in his or her heart, never out loud): "Mirror, mirror, on the wall; am I not the fairest of them all?" The source of this ritual was that ancient desire to be something more than just a reflection, but rather to be the absolute source of all reflections.

Since everyone secretly harbored a hope to be the fairest one of all, most everyone became disturbed if any one of their number, some mere earthperson, began to act as if he or she were the fairest of them all. Disturbance would lead to anger, and anger would boil over into violence.

So it was natural that the young man with the echo in his heart soon became the center of a storm of strife and struggle. But in spite of the hostility he continued to seek some confirmation, some real clarity, that the echo message was not madness.

One evening while at dinner with his friends, he lifted up a cup of wine to drink from it. Looking down into the wine, he saw his own image reflected

86

on its ruby surface — he saw his true self. At that moment he saw something he had never seen before; he saw clearly his own inner-person reflected in the blood-red wine, illuminated by the golden glow of the flickering oil lamps. From his dark reaches erupted the ancient urge of all earthpeople: "Mirror, mirror, am I not the fairest of them all?" From the deepest depths of that cup of wine came the same voice that he had heard as a child. Although not a single friend in the room heard the voice, it spoke so clearly and passionately that its message shattered his heart. But now the ancient taboo had been broken by the earth-man, and immediately, as he raised his eyes from the cup, looking at those he loved so deeply, he realized the price he was about to pay.

For to see your *true* image is indeed to lose your soul.

The End

. . . but not really. For, contrary to the ancient belief, if you see your image — your true image — you do not lose your soul. You may lose a certain level of life, but the life you lose is not your soul. In that death one really finds the true soul, the eternal source and spring, the fountain of life.

What the earthman saw in the magical mirror of his cup was an image filled with unbelievable beauty. The mirror of creation and the mirror of the earth-man now held the same image. And with a mystic smile he handed the cup to his friends and said, "Take this and drink from it . . . . "

The Board Meeting

Recently the press and other media have featured accounts, stranger than fiction, of people who had been pronounced dead and then have come back to life. In almost every case these people tell stories of having experienced great peace and fulfillment and of not wanting to return to life on this earth. These personal accounts of the experience of death and of a return to life hold a special fascination for us who fear death. What follows is an unusual story told to me by a stranger who had just had such an experience.

The stranger began by saying, "I remember resigning myself to the fact that I was dying; I closed my eyes and began to travel down a long, dark tunnel. As I came to the end of it I found myself enveloped in a brilliant light, and as I came through this cloud of light I saw in front of me a large, brick English Tudor manor. The manor was covered with green ivy and had a large oak-timbered front door with great iron hinges. Mounted on the wall to the right of the door was a brass plate that read, 'Private Club, Members Only.' Over the doorway and reaching out to the street upon which I stood was a yellow and white striped canvas canopy. And standing at the front entrance, attired in a scarlet and gold uniform, was a doorman who smiled a warm welcome and opened the door.

"Being unsure that I was a member I hesitated, yet since he continued to hold the door open I decided to go inside the club. I stood in a long hallway whose walls were lined in dark walnut paneling. On

88

the wall was a procession of golden-framed paintings, most of them picturing old, bearded men. A beautiful, red and maroon Persian carpet, a hand's width thick, was at my feet. I walked down a hallway at the end of which I saw a brass-bordered bulletin board mounted on a stand. On it a single announcement read, 'Board of Directors Meeting Today.' Beyond the sign was a huge, open common room. It had a high, timbered ceiling and, like the hallway, had walls of dark walnut. At the far end of the room was a large, brick fireplace. The room was furnished with high-backed, leather easy chairs. Most of the chairs were occupied by elderly folks, although here and there could be seen a young person. Everyone in the room sat in silence, read, or visited with another member in quiet tones. The large room had about it a hushed reverence, the type that's found in banks or churches. Servants in formal dress moved about the room offering drinks and hors d'oeuvres from silver trays.

"At the far end of the club was a circle of easy chairs around a blazing fire. Apparently this was the meeting place of the board of directors. Peels of laughter came from that circle, and since it seemed to be the only lively spot in the otherwise dull room, I walked over toward the fireplace. I pulled up an empty chair to a position on the outside of the circle. As I sat down I discovered the identity of the members of the board of directors, who were exchanging conversation and sipping drinks from clear-bottom pewter mugs. Here is where my tale becomes more fantastic than fiction.

"In the great chair directly across from me sat the Buddha! He was wearing, quite astonishingly, a yellow straw hat — the type made famous by W. C. Fields. On the chair to his right sat the prophet Mohammed who had on his head, of all things, a Mickey Mousekateer hat, the one with the large,

89

black ears. To the left of Buddha sat Moses. He wore a tall, black top hat, the kind worn by diplomats or heads of state. To the left of Moses sat Jesus, who was wearing one of those multicolored, medieval jester's caps, the type with long cloth tails tipped with silver bells. Every time Jesus laughed the bells would ring. Directly in front of me was the highest backed chair, but because of my position I could not see who was sitting there.

"The four men whom I could see were telling jokes, laughing and having a marvelous time. Mohammed, with a twinkle in his eye, was kidding Jesus about the bells on his jester's cap, saying that it was only right that Jesus should have such a cap since his followers were always ringing bells. 'Oh, all those bells,' said Mohammed, 'they hurt your ears.' As he said this he put his hands over the large ears on his Mickey Mouse cap. Again, an avalanche of laughter slid across the circle. Moses then took off his top hat, and reaching inside he drew out a white rabbit who began to do an Israeli folk dance around the brim of the top hat.

"What was most unusual to me about all this was the fact that no one else in the room seemed to hear or notice the humor and laughter. Everyone outside the circle continued to sit in somber silence as those in the circle applauded Moses' dancing rabbit. 'Well done, brother Moses,' grinned Jesus, 'you always know how to unlock a good laugh.'

" 'That's right,' added Buddha as he reached up above his straw hat for his halo and began to spin it around on his index finger, 'and what Jesus just said reminds me of what I saw on a tombstone the other day as I looked down on the state of Rhode Island. Written on the burial stone of a man named Smith were the words:

A zealous Lock-Smith died of late

and did arrive at heaven's gate.
He stood without and would not knock,
because he meant to pick the lock.'

"The others burst into laughter, and Buddha, with a flick of the wrist sent his halo whirling around the circle like some golden frisbee. 'Excellent, brother Buddha,' responded Jesus to the trick, 'but will you look at the people in this room! Just look at the members of our club — so unrelaxed, so proper, and trapped in so much ritual. All of them are so stiff and formal. This place looks more like a mortuary than a club!' At that, Jesus stood up and shouted, 'Awake, the Kingdom is at hand; lift up your eyes and . . . . '

" 'Sit down, brother Jesus,' said Mohammed, 'they can't hear you. Your words are lifeless as far as they are concerned; your words do not awaken any more.'

" 'Mohammed's right,' added Moses. 'Your words, Buddha's, mine — they've all become prisoners. And because they are prisoners, they are without effect. Long ago — for what, at the time, may have been good reasons — people stopped telling the sacred stories, stopped repeating our words . . . and they began to print them in books. Books have become the prisons that hold our words. Our words, filled with passion and devotion — even with a touch of madness — are now incarcerated in great, leather-bound jails called books. Look over there at those bookshelves. The *Tao Te Ching*, the *Koran*, the *Torah*, the *Gospels*, the *Dhammapada*: all imprisoned!'

" 'Yes,' said Buddha, 'our words, once alive and dynamic, a tradition passed on from parent to child, from master to disciple, always fluid — an adjective added here, some color added there to underscore the meaning — were always alive. But as long as they are frozen onto pieces of paper, how can they liberate?'

" 'Only the free can liberate,' added Jesus. 'Oh,

91

how I wish that my words were free, unrestricted and not glued to some paper or scroll. Sacred words should not be memorized but remembered. When they are remembered they pass through the unique prism of each person. As they are retold they come forth alive with energy. They become enfleshed, and only words made flesh can challenge the human heart to greatness.'

" 'Look at those bookshelves,' said Buddha. 'Next to the books that hold our words prisoner are the commentaries, words about our words and thoughts. And next to them are the commentaries on the commentaries, reflections by scholars, dissecting our words to make them more understandable — as though our words were too complex.'

"Laughter bubbled up from the board of directors, and Jesus raised his hand signaling to the waiter, who passed around a tray of fresh drinks. As they sipped their drinks, their eyes scanned the tall, stately shelves of books that lined the walls. Moses broke the silence as he said, 'Poor, silent words sitting alone in their cellblocks of printer's columns: all correctly spelled, the grammar in each sentence precise, every punctuation mark in its proper place. Gray, lifeless words — incarcerated Divine Beauty.'

" 'And,' added Mohammed, 'they are imprisoned without any possibility of bail. Our words stand awaiting trial or, in the case of some, stand already convicted as useless, impotent or trite. And some of our words have even been judged as criminal or insane.' Then, facing the person who sat in the chair directly in front of me and who as yet had not spoken, Mohammed said, 'And all these words are your words.'

"No reply came from the person in the chair, only silence. The silence lasted quite a long time, till Moses cleared his throat, and Mohammed blew his

92

nose on a large, red farmer's handkerchief.

"Slowly, as if it were a great cloud of fog, light began to surround the chair. The cloud of light — almost tangible and filled with a delicious air — spread outward in all directions. Then out of the cloud a voice spoke: 'Jesus, you and your brothers must not be so hard on the other members of the club. They are stiff and unfree because that is how they heard my words. They learned about me and how to behave from the keepers of my words. But the keepers are imprisoned too. It's the old domino principle. And so, it is no wonder that the club is so lacking in spontenaity, in spirit and in humor. I need someone to set my words free, to help them escape. Well, which one of you will go this time?' None of the four responded, and the voice continued, 'I need someone to be a New Word, someone to engineer the biggest jailbreak in history: first to help all my words escape from books and then to show people how to eat my words. I did that once before, with your brother Ezekiel. However, that was a long time ago, and people have forgotten that simple trick.'

" 'My plan this time,' the voice went on, 'is to have a new messiah who will show them how to keep my words free from the prisons of books. Once my words are taken inside, made flesh and remembered, repeated and lived out, then will laughter return. Well,' the voice inquired again, 'which one of you will go this time?'

" 'No thanks,' said Moses, 'I've done my duty; once is enough, if you know what I mean.' Jesus, Buddha and Mohammed all shook their heads in agreement.

" 'Yes, you're right,' responded the voice. 'I can understand how all of you feel. You, Jesus, and you, Mohammed, Moses and Buddha — each of you has already given all that you are. Yes, once is enough.'

"A long empty pause followed these last words, and then a strange thing happened — stranger than all the experiences that I have related to you thus far. The great high-backed chair in front of me began to swivel around. And as it did, the intensity of the light became overpowering. Blinded by the brilliance, I covered my eyes, but even with that the light streamed through my tightly closed eyelids. And out of the light came the voice. It was filled with affection and tenderness, 'Will you, my beloved, will you go?' "

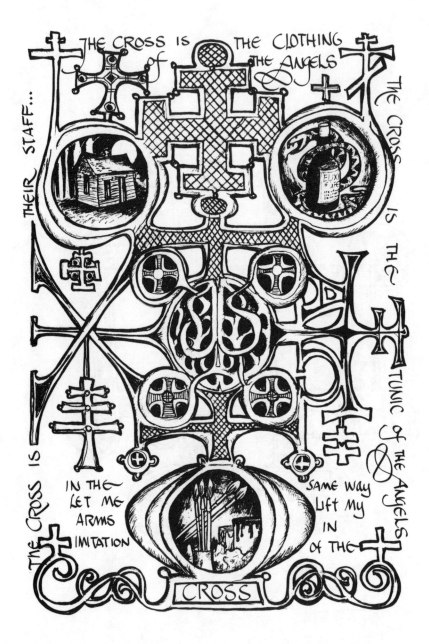

THE CROSS IS THE CLOTHING of THE ANGELS

THEIR STAFF...

THE CROSS IS THE TUNIC OF THE ANGELS

THE CROSS IS IN THE LET ME ARMS IMITATION

SAME WAY LIFT MY IN OF THE

CROSS

The Banduristy

During the oppressive days of Joseph Stalin's dictatorial rule of the Soviet Union, countless acts of brutality and imprisonment were committed. In the mid-1930's Stalin ordered a Congress of Folk Music. Since time immemorial a group of blind folk-singers and story-tellers had wandered up and down the roads of the Ukraine. The great Russian composer, Shostakovich, called them "a living museum, the country's living history." These blind folk-singers were called "the Banduristy," and Stalin gathered several hundred of them from the remote, tiny villages of Russia. When they were all together, he ordered them shot to death! Within one day he had erased a timeless culture with its priceless songs, poetry, legends and stories. Around such a terrible event, naturally, there are countless stories; this one takes place on the evening of that tragic day itself.

The captain's green army uniform was still neat and clean, even though the day had been long and dirty. Darkness now surrounded the tiny peasant's hut that had been recently commandeered as head-quarters. The officer sat at a small wooden table; across from him sat another man. On the table was a flickering oil lamp that cast strange shadows upon the rough log walls of the cabin. Also on the table was a half-empty bottle of vodka, a tin cup, an official-looking letter and a large, black army revolver.

The captain's dark brown hair, while cut short,

97

was still visible beneath his military cap. The old man who sat across from him was white-bearded and dressed in coarse peasant's clothing. After a long period of silence the officer spoke, "You understand, comrade, that what happened out there today was ordered by Generalissimo Stalin." As he spoke he held up the official document, and then slowly set it back on the table. "Would you care for some vodka?"

The old man said nothing; his silence hammered on the walls of the hut. The officer took a drink from the tin cup, lit a cigarette and then blew a white umbrella of smoke upward into the dark shadows of the timbered ceiling. Once again he spoke, "Comrade, you may wonder why you were not executed with those others. It is almost night and my men are tired, that's true. But that is not the real reason I told them that I would, myself, complete the order and dismissed them. When we finish our brief conversation, it will be necessary for me to complete my mission, but I am curious — why do you think that I did not have you killed with the other folk-singers?" Again the old man made no response. "I know you are blind, old man; are you deaf as well?" asked the captain, his voice rimmed with impatience. "Don't you realize that I have the power of life and death over you?"

"You're a young man, aren't you, sir?" replied the folk-singer. His voice was clear, its sound was like silver bells hanging from the harnesses of horses that pull the sleighs in winter. "I would doubt that you are more than twenty-five years old — so young to shoulder so much shame and guilt."

"What shame, what guilt?" snapped the officer. "As a captain in the Soviet Army, comrade, it is often necessary to kill in times of peace as well as war."

"Necessary, sir," questioned the old man, "to kill harmless, blind singers so that progress is not hindered by memories of the past?"

"A good officer, comrade, does not question his orders. If our revolution is to succeed, all orders must be obeyed without question. How else can the liberation of the masses be achieved?"

"Ah, liberation," the old folk-singer returned quietly as if speaking to the wind. "Liberation, freedom, equality of the peoples, a classless society — all hollow words. Are we — are you — in possession of more freedom today than when we lived under the Czar? Are you, my young captain, free *not* to kill me?"

"Enough!" shouted the officer as he smashed his fist to the table. The oil lamp jumped from the force of his blow, causing the strange shadows to suddenly dance crazily upon the walls. "I should shoot you this very moment for such traitorous words about the revolution. If those others, your fellow banduristy, thought as you do, then they were rightly executed as traitors."

"My friends," said the old man, "were shot, sir, not for treason but rather because of what they saw."

"Don't be stupid, comrade," said the captain, "they were all blind; they saw nothing."

"You are wrong, my young friend," said the old man, his sightless eyes penetrating the space where the captain sat. "These men saw what eyes cannot see. That's why they were so dangerous to Stalin. We who are blind have other gifts. We know the art of listening, and sound is a prime source of knowledge. The energy of our senses works not in competition but in harmony. Our sense of rhythm and touch is greater than that of others, and perhaps that is why so many of us are singers and musicians. Most of the sense energy that our eyes would normally use can be channeled to the ears, to the fingers or the nose. We *see*, sir, with our other senses. For example, at

this moment, I smell fear. You, captain, are afraid!"
Reaching across the small table, the folk-singer gently touched the face of the young army captain, who did not move to push away the old man's hand but sat rigid in his chair.

"Ah, yes, as I thought," the old folk-singer said, "you are a young man — and I sense that you are beautiful as well. Beauty is of the heart, while hand-someness is only on the surface. The world loves the handsome and the pretty, but real beauty is seen only when the eyes are closed. We banduristy are being killed because we see inside of things; we see too much. As a result, surface tricks cannot fool us. Progress, liberation and the freedom of the masses — these are all blind words for those who cannot really see."

The old man paused for a moment; then he began again in a quiet tone, "I suspect that I have opened a small door in your heart where memories have begun to escape. You did not kill me, captain, because I remind you of a certain banduristy who once lived near your home village. He taught you to see beauty, encouraged your poetry, enchanted you with his songs and stories. He taught you that real beauty is beneath the surface and that God and magic are still alive! Today, alternating with the rifle shots of the firing squad, you began to hear again those folk songs, and once again you were alive."

"Yes," came the tormented voice of the youthful captain as he gently pushed away the banduristy's hand, "yes, you are correct. You remind me of a man I loved more than my own father — the blind folk-singer of our tiny village. But I am confused; I need time to think, to see what I must do."

"If you wish to see," said the old man, "then blow out the lamp or close your eyes, my young friend. From sight comes the knowledge of facts, but from insight comes wisdom. And insight comes from

100

what you sense as you make your cautious way in the dark along the inner paths of your heart. Close your eyes — feel your way — and then the inner transformation will begin."

The officer leaned forward and blew out the lamp; then he leaned back and closed his eyes. Once again, after many years, the young man remembered the stories and heard the folk songs. He found himself standing in the crowded village church. Great white clouds of incense rose up, out of which appeared the noble faces of the holy ones pictured in the golden icons which glistened in the flickering lights of hundreds of candles. The ancient hymns of the choir rose and fell, a harmony of voices and bells like some eternal earthquake that seemed to swell from the soul of all humanity. Lost in the embrace of his thoughts, he was unaware that the old man was softly singing the ancient Easter hymn, *Allelulia, Christ is Risen.* "The old man is right," thought the captain, "I did love that old folk-singer. I loved the smell and feel of those days, so rich in dreams and ideals. Today, my head is that of a Communist, but my soul — my soul is Russian."

With a resounding crash the night wind blew open the door, banging it loudly against the wall. Through the open doorway, the night wind, smelling of moist spring rain and of fresh death, rushed into the darkened cabin. The captain opened his eyes. His right hand touched the revolver that lay on the table. He remembered now who he was, and he remembered his orders and the revolution — and he was sick with sadness. He did not move to close the door but sat with his hand resting on the revolver. By the light of the spring full moon he could see that the old man was serenely smiling.

"Aren't you afraid to die?" asked the captain.

"My young friend, when you begin to see, then

you learn that death only happens outside and never within you," replied the old singer. "No, I am not afraid to die, nor am I afraid of Stalin or of all the Stalins of history. You can kill the story-tellers, but you cannot kill the story! Others will rise up and take our places. Indeed we need liberty and freedom, but we also need poetry, stories and the liberation of the heart. No, I am not afraid, but you, my young friend, you are afraid. Do not be . . . . "

With that the banduristy rose and began to walk toward the captain. The young man jumped to his feet, picking up the revolver from the table. As they met, the old man warmly embraced the officer, kissing him on the cheek, and he softly began to sing an ancient lullaby: "Do not be fearful, fear not the darkness." The officer struggled to free himself of the embrace of the singer, an embrace that threatened to steal away his sense of reason and his sense of duty. Then suddenly the night air exploded with two gun shots. The smells of gunpowder and blood mingled with the dark aroma of that spring night. For minutes they stood still embracing one another; then with a thud the revolver fell to the floor. Slowly one of them lowered the other to the floor and then slumped into the chair, his head sunk into his hands. The muffled sounds of weeping were wedded to the murmur of the night wind.

At sunrise, a battered old army truck came rattling up the road from the village. A sergeant and two youthful recruits who had arrived that very night came to pick up the captain.

The sergeant, an older man with the face of a peasant, red and rough from years spent out-of-doors in the Russian winters, paused for a moment as he stepped down from the truck. The wind was blowing through the tall cedar trees that bordered the field where the day before he and the other soldiers had

102

planted over three hundred banduristy in the dark soil of Mother Russia. The wind mourned and wailed as it swept across the freshly dug earth and through the tall green cedars. The two young recruits walked behind the sergeant, their gaze riveted on the field with its freshly turned earth. The sergeant stopped as he came to the doorway of the cabin. Caught by the wind the door creaked vacantly. There, in a bright yellow square of sunlight, he first caught sight of the boots — black, polished, military boots — then he saw the green army uniform. The body was face down; the head lay beneath the table. Beside the body was the great, black revolver, an iron island in a pool of blood that had trickled beneath the body.

The old sergeant shook his head and picked up the piece of paper from the table. On the bottom of the military order which was signed with the initials of the captain there was the notation, "Mission completed — the singers have been silenced . . . but not the song."

Placing the paper in the pocket of his tunic, the sergeant said to the two recruits, "Pick him up and give him a decent burial — out there, next to the folksingers, then walk back to the village. I will go and see what I can do to explain this to the commander."

He turned and briskly walked toward the old, battered truck. As he did he thought to himself, "I was afraid this would happen. He was too young to supervise such a slaughter." The sergeant paused before getting into the truck, turning his head to listen. He thought he had heard something, but perhaps it was only the wind in the cedar trees playing tricks on him. He was certain that he had heard, even if faintly, the sound of a folk song being sung somewhere off in the distance, perhaps across the river in the forest. Shaking his head, he climbed into the truck saying to himself, "I must be careful, or I'll be the next one to go." With a loud grinding noise, the old truck's engine came alive.

One of the youthful recruits, a mere lad of fifteen or sixteen, ran to the door of the cabin and called out to his superior. The sergeant, not waiting to listen, thrust his head out the window of the truck and shouted, "I said *bury him*; that's an order!" and with that he drove off down the road toward the village.

The young soldier stepped back into the cabin and said, "I just thought he should know. I think it is very unusual."

"I too, comrade," replied his companion. "Never before have I seen an officer in the Soviet Army with a white beard and of such ancient age."

The Medicine Man

Saturday afternoon in the small, southern county seat was always the same — it was shopper's day. Farmers, as well as the townspeople, used it as the time to purchase supplies for the coming week. The general store, the barber shop, the sales barn — all the stores were busy. The grey-stone, gothic courthouse stood in the center of all the hustle and bustle taking place in the turn-of-the-century buildings that faced it on all four sides. On the tree-shaded lawn of the courthouse old men with black canes sat on the green wooden benches, and children played around the Civil War monument.

Everything was as usual on one particular Saturday afternoon, until suddenly the air was electrified by the sound of circus music. Slowly approaching the town square — towed by a battered, blue van — came a large, brightly painted, old-fashioned medicine wagon. Behind the medicine wagon came a small troupe of colorfully dressed jugglers and tumblers who were dancing in step to the intoxicating blend of circus and country-western music. The music which apparently came from a calliope inside the wagon was magnetic. It drew shoppers from the market, customers left the barber shop, and old men abandoned their benches till a great parade of people was following behind the medicine wagon and its parade of performers.

The medicine wagon, painted with strange, ancient symbols and murals of mystical places like Egypt and India, turned into the parking lot of Craig's IGA store, located one block south of the

105

town square. Within moments the tumblers and jugglers had unfolded a small stage on the rear of the wagon and they erected two flag poles with orange and blue pennants that fluttered gaily in the afternoon breeze. As the crowd surrounded the small stage, the jugglers entertained with clever acts. The crowd was delighted with the surprise of the Saturday afternoon, free entertainment. With a roll from hidden drums and a fanfare from the calliope, through the red and gold curtains on the back of the medicine wagon there stepped onto the stage — the medicine man! The crowd was held in a certain awe, for he was a mysterious-looking man, a commanding, dark-bearded figure. He wore a turquoise-blue tuxedo, complete with a tall, black, silk top hat. With a wide smile he began, "Friends and neighbors, step a bit closer please. I am the medicine man. I have come to your fair city to bring you the Eternal Elixir of Life, a natural laxative, a cure for your itches and pains. Drink this elixir, which has been distilled from the most precious of all the known fluids in the world, and you . . . and you will be freed and healed. Each of you — man, woman and child — has your aches and pains, your fears, worries and problems, but this small medicine bottle contains the source of your liberation."

Some of the city's merchants who were standing in the back row of the crowd smiled and whispered to one another, "I wonder if we could get this guy to come to town every Saturday; think of the crowds he would draw." Standing behind the shopkeepers in a tight, black knot were the members of the local ministerial alliance. They stood silent, somber and stiff as they watched the medicine show.

The medicine man, who radiated charm with every movement, now called the town's sheriff to the stage and asked to be handcuffed. The sheriff secured

106

the medicine man's hands behind his back and then stepped aside with a confident grin. Then, as if on cue, the calliope blared out its mechanical tune as the handcuffed medicine man whirled around and around. When the music stopped, the medicine man came to a rest and raised his arms high in the air. The handcuffs were nowhere to be seen! With a flourish he lifted the sheriff's hat and removed the handcuffs to a roar of laughter and applause from the crowd. The merchants also applauded and said, "What a performer! What a trickster! Now there's a man we can do business with."

"Friends, please step closer to the stage," began the medicine man again, holding a bottle of elixir in his right hand. "Why suffer any longer? Why seek cures where they cannot be found? Take home my ancient and secret medicine, brewed from the most precious fluids found on earth, and know relief from the pains of the body and soul! Pain in the lower back, rheumatism . . . you know, friends, rheumatism is like religion, once you get it you're never comfortable again." The crowd laughed loudly, and the merchants chuckled behind their hands. The ministers, however, exchanged dark glances and shook their heads.

"Or take body itch," continued the chant of the medicine man, "nothing more painful, nothing so robs you of peace and contentment — except, of course, for shoppers itch! You know *that* itch, don't you? You get it every time you enter a store; it's the itch to buy something — anything! You get shopper's itch because of all that merchandise spread out before you. In the old days, when the merchandise was kept behind the counter or in boxes, you went to a store looking for what you really needed and not just something to relieve the itch."

Now it was the shopkeepers' turn to look upset

and shake their heads. Within minutes the two groups were one, as the ministers and the merchants discussed what to do with this rabble-rouser. Soon a note was sent to the stage which read, "You're good at tricks, so disappear — your show is over!" The medicine man read the note and smiled. With uplifted faces the people edged nearer the stage as he announced, "I have been requested by the city fathers to perform for you a daring and most dangerous feat. With your kind permission, ladies and gentlemen, I will disappear!" The audience was all attention as a large, black steamship trunk was placed on the stage. The medicine man, with a flourish of his hat, climbed inside. Then the lid was closed and padlocked and the trunk was tightly strapped with heavy iron chains amidst uneasy murmurs from the spectators. Even the sky began to darken and lightning flickered in the distance. Then suddenly the music of the calliope thundered forth as a great cloud of white smoke exploded around the trunk. As it cleared, they unchained and unlocked the trunk. It was empty! A moment of hushed silence followed as the crowd looked about and began to whisper. The curtains at the back of the wagon were thrust open and out jumped the medicine man! As the cheers died down, he bowed and said, "Friends, neighbors, ladies and gentlemen — as I have escaped easily from my imprisonment, so you too can escape from the canker sores of being critical, the diarrhea of non-discipline and the hemorrhoids of anti-heroism. Drink my elixir and be free of these afflictions, of fear and of anything else that causes you pain. Step forward now and get yourself a bottle of the Eternal Elixir."

A voice from the crowd shouted, "How much is it, mister? Or are you giving it away?"

"No, my good friend," answered the medicine man. "The elixir is not free because freedom is not free. But the price, I promise you, is less than the cost of your present condition, less than the cost of the sickness that afflicts your body and soul."

Before the crowd could come forward to purchase the Eternal Elixir, dark clouds gathered overhead and the wind started to rise, blowing swirls of dust through the street. The crowd began to stir, torn between the appeal of the medicine man and the threat of the approaching storm. The ministers and merchants again began to argue about what to do with this trouble-maker. In the midst of all the confusion the medicine man raised a megaphone to his lips and sang out, "Tomorrow morning, friends, we will have a second show on this very spot. Tomorrow you will learn the secret of staying young for life . . . and longer."

With that, the clergy had had enough. All this talk about freedom from fear was unpleasant, but to have a carnival show on *Sunday* morning, that exclusive time set aside for only "their" business — that was just too much. One of them angrily approached the sheriff, "Does this charlatan, this faker, have a license to peddle his wares on the street? Does he have a license for a public show? If not, then arrest him at once." Another minister shouted to the crowd, "Brothers and sisters, tomorrow morning God's word will set you free. Tomorrow, come to church, praise God and be healed!"

The medicine man raised the megaphone and again chanted to the crowd as the calliope played on, its notes twisting in the rising wind. "Good friends, don't look for God in those pious prisons with their hard pews and rosy windows. The so-called spiritual is no closer to the mystery of God than the tangible. Fear not those . . . "

By this time the sheriff and his men were on the stage and had surrounded the medicine man. The sky grew black and heavy; suddenly the wind became completely still and an uneasy calm fell upon the town. That silence lasted but a moment and was shattered by the long, banshee wail of a tornado siren. With cries of alarm the crowd ran for the safety of the storm shelter in the basement of the county courthouse. In the confusion the jugglers and tumblers quickly piled into their van and fled down the alley, leaving the medicine wagon — and the medicine man — behind. As the sheriff and his men began to rush their prisoner toward the courthouse, the ministers stepped directly in front of their path and said, "He's not to be taken with the others to the shelter. He's too dangerous; they've already heard enough of his atheistic nonsense. Put him over there 'til the storm's passed; then we'll deal with him." They pointed across the street to a house behind which was an old, civil defense bomb shelter. Through the wind-driven clouds of dust and leaves, the sheriff and his men hustled the medicine man to the shelter. Opening its door they pushed him ahead. He stopped, and turning, he smiled calmly and said, "Friends, you can't hold me unless I let you." "That's what you think," said a deputy, giving him a rough shove down the steps. The prisoner crashed downward, striking his head on the last step. Slowly a small pool of blood formed around his head. "He's dead," said one of the men who had rushed down to feel the medicine man's pulse. "I didn't mean to hurt him," whined the deputy who had pushed him, "but he was egging me on." "Don't worry," snapped the sheriff with a worried look at the body, "we'll say it was an accident, that he slipped. It's not our fault; it's those damn' ministers and merchants that wanted him shut up. Come on, be quick about it, or we'll be dead too. Lock him in here, and we'll do something about it when the storm has passed."

110

The full force of the wind and the rain pelted them as they slammed shut the heavy door, padlocked and chained it, and then ran for the courthouse basement. The storm raged most of the night with violent winds and raging rains. As they huddled together, the people pondered the mysterious words of the medicine man. It was only with the first light of dawn that the all-clear siren blew, and the people began to come out of the basement shelter. By the light of the rising sun they could see that the main force of the storm had missed the town. There were a few trees blown down and minor damage here and there, and in the IGA parking lot the medicine wagon had tipped over on its side. The people thanked God for their safety and rejoiced in the fresh air of this new day. One of the merchants announced to the crowd, "Since our business was interrupted yesterday afternoon, we will open our doors immediately after church this morning to serve you and your needs." One of the ministers chimed in, "Yes, yes, church as usual this morning; come this way, brothers and sisters . . . . " But a strange thing happened. The people began to drift away quietly, not toward the church but to their homes and farms.

Meanwhile, the sheriff and his men, with a delegation of the merchants and ministers, approached the old bomb shelter. Terror grasped them when they found the heavy door torn off at its hinges. Peering fearfully inside they found only the medicine man's tall, black, silk top hat and turquoise tuxedo — neatly folded in a corner. Other than these, the underground shelter was completely empty.

Across the street in the parking lot of the IGA store, the medicine man's wagon lay on its side, one wheel slowly revolving. Without any warning, the calliope began to play a slow, haunting melody. Beyond fright, the sheriff and those with him ran across the street to the medicine wagon. Looking inside they could find no calliope nor any other source of music. They saw only box upon box of the Eternal Elixir.

The sheriff took one bottle from a box, broke the seal, smelled the contents, and then poured some of the fluid into the palm of his hand. Then he dabbed a little on his fingertip and raised it to his lips.

"Well, sheriff, what is it; what's in all these bottles?" asked one merchant, speaking for them all. The sheriff's face was pale. He looked at his finger and then across the street toward the empty bomb shelter, and in a trembling voice he said, "It's blood!"

The Revolutionary

This tale of conflict and courage takes place in a small Central American country. It was a land marked by the lush, green foliage of its mountainous jungles, by the gleaming, white buildings of its capital city — whose centerpiece was a beautiful, stately, old Spanish cathedral — and by an ever-present, steaming heat. For twelve months of the year the tropical heat was oppressive, and the life of the country was lethargic. But the constant heat was not the only reason for this national listlessness, for the country was ruled by an equally oppressive military dictatorship. Many years ago a group of army officers had successfully carried off a bloodless coup d'etat and now ruled the country by a right-wing military junta.

The small national army was equipped with hand-me-downs from a neighboring superpower in whose chain of defense this small country was considered an important link. Since the days when political power had been seized from a corrupt dictator, business had improved greatly. With the national life now stable, tourists came by the thousands. To the casual eye of the tourist everything seemed peaceful and orderly — even democratic. However, there was only one radio station, one newspaper and one television channel, each of which was owned and operated by the government, a government formed by the only political party allowed. The complete control exercised by the present dictatorship was carefully camouflaged but was as ever-present and as harsh as the heat. No public opposition to the ruling junta could be spoken or written.

The economic system also supported the oppression. Bank loans were at a very low rate of interest, and so most of the people, the great majority of whom were very poor, were constantly in debt. Since numerous loan payments hung over the heads of the workers, they were never anxious to go on strike. The military government also strongly encouraged any traditions that were suited to its ends, in particular the old native custom of boys and girls being married by the age of sixteen. The leaders knew that once people have spouses and small children, they become less likely to engage in acts of political unrest. There was also the government's ploy of giving each family that lived near the capital city a free television set and those who lived in the jungles a transistor radio. Since the junta controlled the media, the people were thus constantly indoctrinated through the official entertainment and news. Furthermore, the secret police, by means of informers, made sure that no political unrest was aroused in the countryside or in the cities. Every now and then people would "disappear" in order to set an example. Months later they would be found dead — their bodies mutilated by the torture of the secret police. The people thus understandably lived in constant fear of the secret police and of being arrested as an enemy of "law and order." So total was the junta's domination.

It should be noted, however, that not everyone was passive under the oppression, for hidden in the mountains were small bands of revolutionaries. Their ranks were composed mainly of non-married men and women who had left their homeland to be educated in the countries to the north. Upon their return they spoke out loudly against the tyranny of the ruling junta. In time they were forced to flee to the mountains as fugitives of the law. As they were relatively few in number and poorly armed, their effectiveness was limited. On occasion they would strike out — a bridge blown up here, an army outpost attacked there — but for the most part they were powerless to overthrow the strong government.

Not every young person who had gone north to study, however, returned to become a gun-carrying revolutionary. There was one young man who had gone away to study art and returned to live a quiet life at his home in one of the small, remote villages. He was ordinary yet in a way extraordinary, friendly yet somehow distant. Like many of the men in his country he did not attend church, but he was deeply religious and prayerful. The paintings of this quiet young man were of local scenes and of very common things. But from them there came a feeling — a spirit — of freedom as well as great beauty. Many of the peasants did not understand the paintings, but they always felt that sense of being liberated whenever they saw them. The colors and even the forms were luminous, and light seemed to radiate outward from the paintings. The poor and oppressed people would walk for miles simply to look at them and left feeling once again like free men and women. The military government, concerned about the painter's popularity, sent the secret police to examine his work. They returned to report that the paintings were only pretty pictures of ordinary things, but the junta remained apprehensive.

Meanwhile, the Church had also taken notice of the young artist. A delegation of clergy came from the capital city to offer him a commission to paint large murals on the walls of the cathedral. Since the time they were built, several centuries ago, the walls had remained bare of any decoration. Actually, the church leaders were concerned that so few people were attending church services any longer, and they hoped that by engaging the popular painter the people would once again begin to come back to church. The young artist, with a smile and a bow to the reverend clergy, eagerly accepted the commission.

Over the months that followed, with swift execution, a series of fantastically beautiful murals began to take shape on the once bare walls of the old cathedral. The frescoes spoke of a God of justice and mercy. They did not reveal a majestic cosmic ruler but rather a God of the poor and oppressed. For example, in a mural of the exodus from Egypt, God was depicted as one of the slaves building the pyramids. When asked by the priest-rector of the cathedral why he had represented God in such a strange way, the quiet artist replied, "In the beginning, Father, God was a friend of those treated unjustly, of the poor, the widow and the orphan. But gradually over the centuries, the image of God changed to that of a judge of the people rather than their protector. Instead of being one with the oppressed, the Divine Presence was pictured as a king, as part of the ruling class. In the ancient days, Father, holiness was not so much to be found in church attendance or in acts of piety but rather in doing deeds of justice for the weak and wronged."

The flabby, colorless priest only smiled and said, "That's nice, my son, but aren't you going to paint a beautiful Madonna?"

Listening was a large crowd of the poor people. Barefoot, they stood gazing upward in wonder at the giant murals with their radiant colors. The murals seemed to have not only a luminous but a liquid quality; they were fluid yet firmly stable. Like his paintings in the village, there was about these murals that intangible sense of freedom and rightness. Each day, more and more of the people flocked to the old cathedral to watch the painter and to see the murals. Even if the pudgy rector of the cathedral did not comprehend the message of the murals, the military junta did!

The young artist lived as simply here in the capital as he had in his native village. He had been granted permission to sleep on the roof of the cathedral. One night as he lay under the stars, he was visited by the secret police. They warned him that unless the style and content of his paintings were changed he would be arrested and dealt with accordingly. The painter merely listened in silence to their orders. The next morning, he continued painting as though the dark threat had vanished with the coming of the dawn.

Within a week, crews of soldiers marched into the cathedral and began to whitewash the newly painted murals. Undaunted, the young artist moved to the west wall of the cathedral and began to paint a Madonna. But as the days passed a strange thing happened. The murals began to reappear slowly through the soliders' white paint. This had an almost enchanting effect on the crowds that daily filled the cathedral. The poor now came not only to see the magical murals but also just to be in the presence of this strange and prayerful painter.

The mural of the Madonna was immense and striking. She was serene and beautiful, pictured as a young native woman with dark skin and dark black hair. But what drew the larger interest of the great crowds was the background of the painting. Behind the blue-and-white robed Madonna was a series of small pictures that told a story. They illustrated a colony of ants who, speck by speck, were eating away at a tall, fortress-like tower. Finally, the tower crashed to the ground and in so doing crushed a church resembling the very cathedral of the capital city. Also, in the lap of the Madonna was a Christ-child holding a scroll that read, "Unless a grain of

117

wheat falls to the earth and dies, it remains just a grain of wheat. But if it dies, it produces much fruit."

As the young painter worked high atop the scaffolding, hastening to finish the Madonna, he thought about the offers he had received to join the mountain revolutionaries. He had declined their invitations and knew that the revolutionaries did not understand his refusal to join them. But he also knew that the hour of darkness was coming, and he had to invest his energy where it was to do the most good. In the midst of these musings, he felt the pulsing presence of the Divine Mystery — faceless, unknowable and unreachable — yet without any doubt, real and present. His thoughts were broken by the sharp, loud command of an army officer who ordered the cathedral to be vacated. Within minutes the painter was arrested and taken away to the national security prison.

The military authorities did not want to give the people a martyr, and so they did not kill the painter but tortured him instead. Each day, the secret police removed one of his fingers until his hands were only mutilated stumps. Weeks later, he was found unconscious on the front steps of the cathedral. They released him so that he would be a walking sign of what would happen to anyone else who might oppose them. However, the officials had failed to imagine the effect that the mutilation of the painter would have on the people. The news spread quickly through the city and the countryside. The next day the poor took to the streets, first by the hundreds, then by the thousands. Shoulder to shoulder, the faceless, unimportant common people filled the dusty avenues that led to the cathedral square. All work ceased; all shops were closed.

The military commanders ordered their troops into action. As the silent thousands entered the cathedral square, they came face to face with ranks and ranks of well-armed soldiers. As the officer in charge gave the command for the crowds to disperse, the voice of the painter could be heard from the roof of the cathedral, "Fear not, God is with you. God is always the champion of the weak and the oppressed." The crowd, now fearless, moved forward to vollies of gunfire. The sound of rifle shots and the cries of the wounded united with the shouts of "Freedom" as the masses of poor rushed the machine guns. As the battle in the streets reached its peak, the armed revolutionaries from the mountains poured into the city. Within an hour the tide of the struggle changed, and now the people were in control. They captured the national security prison and burned it to the ground after setting everyone free, and they seized the presidential palace. Many of the leaders of the government were killed in the fighting and others took their own lives. The angry mobs were able to capture six officers of the ruling junta as they were attempting to escape wearing civilian clothing.

The enraged citizens, led by the head of the revolutionary army, were filled with revenge and a thirst for justice. They demanded the death of all their oppressors. The young painter now came forward and exclaimed that, while these men had been cruel and unjust, the new government should treat them with mercy. His quiet voice, however, was lost in the angry shouts of those whose relatives had been raped, tortured or murdered. Those who had lost much demanded that justice be swift and painful. The revolutionary leader responded by stating that all those captured would be shot before dawn of the next day.

Pleading for mercy, the condemned men were dragged away to the basement of the presidential palace where they were to be held for the night since the prison had been destroyed. Their cries for mercy continued until shortly after midnight when strangely their voices became silent. Meanwhile, the entire city celebrated its freedom as fireworks illuminated the night sky. The streets were crowded with dancing people who made merry with rum and song long into the night.

The revolutionary leader, now the new president of the country, slept that night in the ex-president's ornate bed. He had celebrated so much that he overslept the appointed hour of the execution. Since the officer in charge was still drunk, a young revolutionary officer, who had arrived only that night from the mountain hide-out, took command of the firing squad. The young officer felt that he must carry out the orders as they were written, "execution of the enemies of liberty and the revolution shall take place before sunrise." So, he ordered the condemned men to be taken from the basement and lined up against the tall, white courtyard wall of the palace.

Seven men walked across the dew-covered, darkly shadowed lawn as the first pink shades of dawn were touching the sleeping city. Something was quite different about the condemned army officers. They walked with a sense of dignity. It was not that they seemed courageous, for courage is strength in the face of fear; rather, they seemed to be altogether without fear. The condemned men, dark silhouettes against a white wall, waited with a calm nobility. A loud volley of shots shattered the pre-dawn darkness as one of the condemned shouted, "May God be with you as well!"

The new president was awakened by the rifle shots and staggered slowly out of bed. He kicked an empty wine bottle from beneath his feet as the woman in the spacious bed rolled over and returned to sleep. As he descended the wide marble staircase and was strapping on his gun belt and holster, the young officer rushed up the first steps and saluted, "Sir, orders carried out as they were given: all seven of the army officers have been executed."

"Seven," grunted the sleepy president, "where did you find the other one hiding?"

"Sir, there were seven when we brought them from the basement," replied the junior officer.

The two men walked across the vast green lawn, now touched by the golden light of the rising sun, while off in the distance the cathedral bells were ringing to announce early Mass. The executed men had fallen face down on the lawn, and so the president examined each of the dead by rolling them over with the toe of his boot. When he came to the seventh and last man, however, he did not roll him over. Looking at his hands, he saw that there were no fingers — only mutilated stumps!

On the other side of the capital city which was now slowly awakening after its wild and drunken celebration, the rising sun shone through the great rose window in the east wall of the cathedral. A single ray of light, yellow-white and dazzling, streaked across the long nave, touching the mural of the Madonna on the west wall. Like a laser beam, the ray of the sun was focused on the scroll held by the Christ-child, illuminating its message: "Unless a grain of wheat falls to the earth and dies, it remains just a grain of wheat. But if it dies, it produces much fruit."

Hanna's Harmonica

The radio, that Sunday morning, had predicted that the temperature would climb to 103 degrees and that it would be one of the hottest August thirds in the history of the city. The temperature at 9 o'clock was already 88, and rising, as Hanna began to cross 13th street on her way to church. Hanna was a heavy-set, middle-aged, black woman. This Sunday morning she wore her favorite white dress, and, although a large woman, the dress gave her the appearance of luminous buoyancy. With care for her white high heels she made her way gingerly across the black asphalt street crossing which already had the "feel" of licorice.

Hanna was on her way to the 10 o'clock morning worship at Saint Stephen's Abyssinian Baptist Church. As was her custom, she was taking a short cut through the tiny city park on the other side of which was St. Stephen's. The one square block of park was an oasis of green in the midst of the old, rundown, red-brick apartment houses that bordered it on all sides. In the very middle of the small green park was a giant, old oak tree, perhaps eighty to one hundred feet tall, whose branches spread out wide on all sides, umbrella-like. The narrow footpath passed under the tree's umbrella branches, and on the side of the path, directly across from the giant tree, was a green, wooden park bench.

When Hanna reached the bench she sat down to rest, taking a large, white handkerchief from her purse to wipe her brow. "Sweet Jesus, but it's hot to-day," she said. "Yes," came a reply, "it's summer, you know." Hanna looked around but saw no one. The park was empty at this hour of the morning. She stood up and walked around the tree's grey trunk but could find no one. She sat down again, saying to herself, "Sweet Jesus, Hanna, the heat's gettin' to you!" She then opened her purse again, removing an antique, silver harmonica and began to play it softly. The old harmonica had belonged to her daddy, now dead so many years. The music that Hanna played was a blend of blues and ragtime. As the harmonica's music drifted out across the park, Hanna reflected on the fact that her daddy never went to church during the summertime. On Sunday mornings when she and her mother were off to church, he would sit on their back porch and play his harmonica.

When her mother, a staunch churchgoer, would scold him for staying at home, regardless of how hot it might be, her daddy would only reply, "Preachin' and praisin' the Lord only raises the body heat, and in weather like this the body is hot enough without compoundin' the problem with 'holy' heat!" This Sunday, Hanna wished that SHE could stay home, 'cause it was just too hot to go to church. But her best friend, Ruby Robinson, was sick with cancer, and there was to be a healing service that morning at St. Stephen's. And there was, of course — as always — Leroy! Leroy was her twenty-eight-year-old, late-to-mature, unmarried and unemployed son. Ever since her husband had died, several years ago, she had tried everything — she had prayed, petitioned and pleaded with Leroy. This morning she would add another ring of petitions to her endless chain of prayers for the child.

She put down her silver harmonica, wiping her brow with her handkerchief as she said to herself, "Sweet Jesus, but I wish that they could have church outside here in the park this morning."

124

"Why not?" once again came a mysterious reply. "Sweet Jesus," said Hanna, "what's comin' over me?"

"Incorrect, Hanna," returned the voice, "Jesus is my son, I'm his father." Hanna stared BB-holes of disbelief at the giant tree, as the wind swept gently through the tall upper branches, rustling the green leaves. "That's right, Hanna," continued the voice, "I am who you think I am." This time no "Sweet Jesus" came from Hanna; she only sat stone-still, staring at the great tree.

"I like trees," came the voice again. "In fact, I like them the best of all the things that I've made. And whenever I come to be among my human children, it is one of my favorite forms to take. I like trees. Their branches reach up, touching the heavens, and their roots are sunk deep, deep down in the dark earth. I'm like that, Hanna, half in the earth and half in the heavens. My trees also do the best job of preaching my most important lesson. They are living gospels of summer, autumn, winter and spring. Each winter they die only to come to life again in the spring. Think about that, Hanna, 'cause I'm letting you in on one of the best kept secrets in all history." Then the voice from the tree laughed and laughed.

"You mean," Hanna said, "that God, ah, I mean that *you* are a tree?"

"No," answered the voice, "not exclusively. Over the many years I have been fire, wind, a mountain here and there, and of course, dear, people — special people. But trees — yes, trees — are my very favorite disguises. Remember the Tree of Life in the Garden of Eden? It was also not by accident that my son Buddha reached enlightenment in a forest under a Bo tree in India. And my son Mohammed taught about the Tree of Paradise. And the Druids had their Sacred Oak. And when it came time for my beloved son Jesus to die — I did not abandon him because he was

125

nailed to me. I held him in my wooden arms like a brokenhearted mother. I held him up high so that all the folks could see how much I loved him and how much he loved me."

"Lord God," said Hanna, "I know this ain't no dream 'cause it's too hot here to be a dream. But why are you telling me all these beautiful things?"

God laughed long and hard. "Hanna, it's your music, your harmonica music. It touches my heart. Scott Joplin, isn't it? He's one of my favorites too." Hanna looked down with amazement at her daddy's old harmonica.

The voice went on, "You see, Hanna, laughter and music are the language of heaven — they're MY sounds. All music is sacred, not simply churchy music but all of it: rock and roll, rhythm and blues, country, classical, jazz and ragtime . . . . "

"But Lord," asked Hanna, "why is music your sound? I don't understand. And laughter . . . if laughter is your sound, why don't we hear it in church?"

"Hanna, dearest," said God, "the deepest mysteries are expressed in the most common of ways. Music is not just the handmaid of religion — at its heart it *is* religion. Music is harmony, and whenever you play it or really listen to it you proclaim the mystery of my being. And laughter — that's the language of children . . . and there are no grown-ups in heaven!" Silence followed this statement as Hanna slowly turned these thoughts in her heart.

The voice continued, "All my children are meant to be musicians, for the making of music is the way of returning to me. All my 'special' children were musicians: Krishna and his flute, Pan and his pipes, and Apollo and his harp. And Matthew, Mark and the other two left out an important bit of information about my boy Jesus when they forgot to tell that his

126

mama taught him some real catchy tunes on the shepherd's flute. Not bad on the harp either, but he probably got that from his great-grandfather, David. Remember, Hanna, music is the way of return. Whenever you play music or truly listen to it, you are in me and I am in you."

Hanna raised the old, silver harmonica to her lips, and the ragtime music flowed out, encircling and caressing the great tree. The leaves shimmered and danced upon their delicate stems. Without warning, however, she stopped and began to cry, "Oh, Lord, I'm so happy. I'm so at peace here with you. I just hate it that my God-fearing mama didn't know about daddy's harmonica music — about your sound."

"Don't cry, Hanna," replied the voice from the tree, "she knows now . . . she knows now."

"Lord," asked Hanna, "can I ask you a favor?"

"Sure, Hanna; in fact, according to all the ancient rules of story books, you can ask three favors — any three you wish," replied the tree-voice.

"Well you see, Lord, I was on my way to church this morning to pray over Ruby Robinson. She's real sick and has a big family depending on her. I should be there, over at church, but I hate to leave you. Could you cure her, Lord?"

"Sure, Hanna, whatever you ask," was the reply. At that very moment, not a split second later, there came a great, thunderous shout of praise from St. Stephen's Baptist Church. "There, that's one favor granted; you've got two more to go," said the voice from the tree.

"Lord, it's my boy, Leroy. Find Leroy a hard-working, bible-loving, full-breasted, clean-living and fun-loving woman — and also a good job that he can like and stick to."

"Done," said the tree, "within the day, I promise you. But so far, Hanna, these favors have been for others; don't you have something you want just for yourself?"

Hanna was silent for a long time; then she smiled, "Well, Lord, if I have any wish at all it is that I might be just as happy as this all the days of my life. I love being this close to you, hearing you laugh, listening to your music and your wonderful stories."

The great branches of the tree gently reached down and encircled Hanna as the tree spoke, "Are you sure, Hanna, real sure that this is what you really want . . . to hear my laughter and music like this all your days?"

"Yes, Lord, no doubt about it, I'm positive," she answered.

"Then," said the tree, "so be it. Your favor is granted, and for all of your days you will be in me and I will be in you. You will live forever in my harmony and in the laughter of heaven. That's a promise, Hanna, and I always keep my promises."

It was high noon as the Sunday worshippers poured out of Saint Stephen's sauna and headed for home. A group of ladies from the church were walking together across the little park. They were chatting about the miracle that had happened to Ruby Robinson, and they were also wondering why Hanna hadn't been at church. It wasn't like her to miss church, regardless of the weather. Then, they saw the green park bench and stopped . . . frozen in their footsteps. For neatly draped across the bench was a large, white dress, and beside it, neatly arranged, were a set of undergarments. Beneath the bench were two high heeled, white shoes. The noontime air was overflowing with the rhythm of ragtime, but no musician could be seen anywhere. However, searching for the source of the sounds, they looked up into the branches of the great tree and saw Hanna. She was perched in a crotch made by two huge branches and

128

was playing her harmonica as if she were possessed. All she wore was a smile, a smile as wide as Wyoming!

This is not the end of the story, but almost the end. You should know that Hanna lived for another thirty years after that Sunday and died at the ripe age of eighty-five. She died as she had lived — a happy woman. In fact, those who knew her said that they had never known a happier and more contented woman — even if for the last thirty years of her life she had lived as a patient at the State Hospital for the Insane.

The Hired Hand

L. C. and Ruth had been married about ten years, struggling during that time to bring into the world, clothe, and feed three small children from the income of their farm. It was a small farm, and so L. C. had to drive a school bus as a second means of income. That, together with Ruth's amazing skill at stretching a dollar, made it possible for them to survive. They were always in debt, but, while poor, the family was happy.

One day a man came walking up the dusty lane to the small, white farmhouse. He was in his late twenties or perhaps early thirties. He had long hair and a beard and wore an old army fatigue jacket and faded jeans. As the man approached the porch, L. C. walked out the screen door saying, "What happened, did your car break down?"

"No," replied the stranger, smiling, "in fact, I'm not even driving. I was just passing by and saw a lot of unfinished work around your place and thought that perhaps you might need an extra hand. I'm looking for work."

"You're looking for work," said L. C., "and I'm looking for help, but I'm afraid that's where our mutual needs end. I can barely keep food on the table and shoes on my kids' feet as it is. Sorry, stranger, I'd like to hire you, but I just can't afford to."

"Oh, money's not important to me," said the stranger, "I'd be willing to work just for room and board. I've been on the road for a long spell and need to settle down; need to do some good, hard manual labor. Give me a place to stay and my meals; that'll

130

be enough."

Now L. C.'s heart took a flying leap and turned a somersault because he was behind in his spring planting, and he really needed an extra man around the farm. L. C. looked the stranger over; he looked decent enough, didn't appear to be some tramp. "Here, take a seat while I ask my wife what she thinks," said L. C., pointing to an old, white wicker chair with one broken leg.

L. C. returned about five minutes later and said, "Looks like a deal. Ruth agreed, and we decided that you could sleep in the room up in the attic and have your meals with us. What's one more plate on the table? And we also figured that we can afford to give you about twenty-five dollars a month, sort-a spending money, you might say. When do you want to begin?"

"How about right now?" returned the stranger. "I see you have a pile of firewood that needs splitting."

"Good," said L. C., "let's shake on it, and you can start this morning." And so the two men shook hands. The stranger left his coat on the porch and began to walk toward the woodpile when L. C. came after him. "Excuse me, friend," he said, "I forgot to ask your name."

The stranger stopped, and rolling up his shirt sleeves he turned and smiled, "My name is Jesus Christ; glad to be working for you." Then he turned and walked to the woodpile where he began to swing the axe with powerful strokes. L. C. walked into the house shaking his head. He said to Ruth, "I hope we haven't made a mistake and gotten some weirdo on our hands. Well," continued L. C. after a pause, "if he acts strange we can send him on his way plenty fast."

But the new hired hand did not prove to be a weirdo; in fact, it was just the opposite. He was a

131

steady and hard worker, doing all he was asked and more. He was a friendly but quiet sort of man. L. C., Ruth and the children found that they enjoyed his presence in their home. Right off the bat L. C. gave him the nickname "Jess," saying, "Can't go around called a hired hand 'Jesus'!"

Jess was truly an answer to their prayer for help, even if he did have some strange habits. For example, he never went into town — ever! If he did need anything, he would ask L. C. to pick it up when he went to town. Jess told the family, "I don't like towns very much. I prefer to stay out here where it's quiet and peaceful."

He also had a habit at the table that at first caused the children to giggle. When handed a piece of bread at the beginning of the meal, he would always reverently kiss it. Strangely, after a time, each member of the family picked up this habit, and everyone did it silently right after the meal blessing. When, as so often happens, the conversation at table turned to gossip about who was doing this or that, Jess would always, very cleverly, change the subject or tell some funny story.

Also, when Jess watched TV with the family, L. C. noticed that he sometimes wept quietly. Silent tears would slowly roll down his face whenever there were pictures of killings or of suffering refugees on the evening news. At such times he would excuse himself and leave the room, not returning to watch until it was time for the weather.

The three children loved Jess. He was unlike any other adult they had ever known. When Jess played with them it was as if he were once again a small child lost in the pretending and fantasy of their games. He never treated them as inferiors or talked down to them. Broken dolls and wagon wheels that needed repair were all brought to him, and he told stories to the children as he repaired their toys. But whether told to the children or their parents, Jess's stories were never about himself. He never talked about where he had been, and all that he would say about the future was, "Some day I'm going home to see my father." Ruth and L. C. respected his desire for privacy and never asked questions about his personal life.

He worked hard all week, but on Sundays he would disappear, spending the day walking in the fields and woods. Sometimes he would return around sunset, other times not until way after dark. Jess certainly loved his solitude. When Ruth had asked him if he wanted to go to church with them on Sunday morning, he politely thanked her and said, "No, Ruth, churches tend to make me sick, too closed-in or something, and the sermons usually make me angry. No, it's much better that I stay away. Churches are intended to lead you somewhere that I've found by another way." While not a churchgoer, Jess was a prayerful man — not simply at the table but at other times as well. One night, late, after the kids were asleep, L. C. had stood at the bottom of the stairs leading up to the attic. He could hear, faintly, Jess talking to God. Softly, but with deep tenderness, he prayed, as the flicker of yellow candle light leaked out from beneath the closed attic door.

The months followed each other in rapid procession, and before L. C. knew it almost seven months had passed since Jess had joined the family. All of them, in that short time, had fallen in love with him. He was strong yet gentle, humorous yet serious, kindly but also very firm about the things he would or wouldn't do. One Thursday afternoon, Jess surprised them by asking if he could take the rest of the day off and if he could borrow the pickup truck to go into town. In the previous months Jess had never left

133

the farm, and so L. C. gladly gave him the keys. Jess didn't return for supper that night; in fact, it was well after dark when he finally did come home from town.

The next morning, Friday, L. C. and Jess were repairing the corn picker. It was the middle of November, and the breakdown had put them behind in their work. About mid-morning Jess asked L. C. to come with him to the barn, saying that he had something that he wanted to show him. He led L. C. to the far end of the barn where bales of hay were stacked almost to the roof. Turning a corner, L. C. saw a narrow tunnel-like passageway that led through the walls of hay bales. At the end of the passageway they came to a small room-like opening. A single, wide shaft of yellow sunlight poured through a large crack in the barn boards. It illuminated all sorts of marvelous things: a new bicycle, a tall doll with yellow hair, a red toy wagon and a whole array of other toys. Jess opened a box, revealing a beautiful quilted bathrobe, just Ruth's size. And behind that box was another one with a tag that read simply, "to L. C., the boss-man." Stunned, L. C. slowly sat down on a bale of hay and shook his head. "I don't understand," he said, "where did all this stuff come from?"

"Well," said Jess smiling, "I overheard you telling the kids a few weeks ago that with all the doctor bills due for Ruth's sickness this year, and with the poor price of wheat, that Christmas would be 'just going to church' and that Santa Claus wouldn't be stopping here this year. I sort-a figured, L. C., that if the kids ever needed a Christmas it was this year, what with their mom being sick so much and everything. So, I took the money that you and Ruth have given me over the months and decided to buy these gifts with it. I hope you don't mind, that you don't take offense at what I've done."

L. C. found it difficult to speak, his heart lodged

134

in his throat. "Thank you, Jess; it's so typical of you. Ruth and I thank you for this and for everything else you've done for us. What a blessing it was the day you came to our place. But, Jess, this is only the middle of November. Why are you showing me all these Christmas things now?"

"This morning," answered Jess, "I woke up with this strange feeling that it's time for me to leave here! I can't explain it, I just know that the time has come — today, Friday. Leaving here is not what I would choose; try to understand, please. I love you all, more than you know. I'm sorry, but it's out of my hands now."

L. C. stood up, tears welling in his eyes, and he embraced Jess. Neither man spoke, both aware of how much they loved each other. Unable to put into words what he felt, L. C. turned away, saying softly, "Let's talk about this at lunchtime." He walked through the narrow tunnel in the hay bales and out into the barn. Opening the barn door he saw two blue cars driving up the dusty front lane. Even before they stopped in front of the porch, L. C. recognized the two patrol cars from the sheriff's office. The sheriff and two deputies got out of the first car. The under-sheriff and three recruits, straight from the steps of the county courthouse and armed with shotguns, climbed out of the second car.

"Howdy, L. C.," said the sheriff, "how's your corn crop this year?"

"Fair, sheriff, only fair," answered L. C., "but I'm sure that you didn't come all the way out here with this small army from the county courthouse just to check on my corn crop."

The sheriff, a large man with a politician's grin and a buddha-like belly, smiled and said, "You're right, L. C., I'm on business this mornin'." He removed a photo from a folder and showing it to L. C.

asked, "Ever seen this man before?"

L. C. recognized at once the image of Jess in the photograph, and pausing he replied, "Why do you ask, sheriff?"

"Because, L. C.," responded the sheriff, "he was seen yesterday in town, and he was driving your pick-up!" The men in the circle around L. C. looked at one another. One of them winked at the sheriff, and they all grinned. "I got a warrant for his arrest," the sheriff continued, "so you might as well tell me where he is."

"He's over in the barn," said L. C., "but I can't imagine why you would want him."

"O.K., men," said the sheriff, "let's not take any chances. He may be dangerous so keep your guns ready." The sheriff and his band of men entered the barn, weapons drawn.

Ruth had come out onto the porch. She and L. C. stood there together, paralyzed with unbelief. Within a few moments the officers came out of the barn leading Jess, who was handcuffed. As they ushered him into the back seat of one of the cars, Jess paused briefly and looked toward the porch. His eyes filled with messages, he smiled at L. C. and Ruth. Then, in a moment he was gone, hidden from their view.

The sheriff came up on the porch, and tipping his hat to Ruth said, "Thank you, L. C., for your co-operation. I know that the missus didn't know what sort of man you had here. You both will rest easier now, knowing that he's in safe custody."

"But what," said L. C. haltingly, "what did he do to be arrested? He's the kindest, gentlest man we've ever known. What harm could he have ever done?"

The sheriff smiled another one of his politican's grins — like the one he wore for his election poster — and said, "Here's a note he was writing when we caught him. It's addressed to you." The sheriff handed the folded piece of paper to L. C. and continued, "As for that guy — why L. C., he's nutty as a fruitcake! He escaped seven months ago from the State Insane Asylum! You know, he thinks he's Jesus Christ! Ain't that a laugh? And as far as not being dangerous, why the last time he escaped he busted up this church over by Murdock — chased the congregation out and began busting up the place while the poor minister nearly had a heart attack. He just went berserk, yelling something about prayer, his father's house, and a lot of religious junk. He smashed up the whole dang place with an axe before the law could get there. But nothing to worry about now, we'll see he's behind bars before sunset. He thinks he's Jesus Christ; ain't that a laugh?" With that, the sheriff touched his fingers to the brim of his hat and walked down the steps of the porch. Climbing into his car, he drove down the lane.

The last they saw of Jess was through the rear window of the second car. He had turned around in the back seat for one last look, and once again he smiled — a sad, longing smile. Ruth was crying. She buried her face in her apron as L. C., who was weeping as well, slumped into the battered wicker chair. Through his tears he recognized Jess's handwriting on the note given him by the sheriff. The message on the inside was simply a quotation from the French writer, Pascal: "Men are so necessarily mad that not to be mad would amount to another form of madness."

The Suitcase

This unusual affair could have happened to anyone, but it happened to a young man named Sam. Each morning Sam would ride with a friend to work, meeting him at a place along the side of the highway. One particular morning, as he walked along his usual shortcut through a patch of woods on his way to the main highway, the normal pattern of his day was disrupted. As Sam approached the middle of the woods, he was surprised to see a large brown suitcase sitting beside a huge, old tree. Sam stopped to look at the brown leather suitcase which appeared to be in good condition. It was of excellent craftsmanship and was made of real leather. "This suitcase is too expensive to have been thrown away," Sam thought. "Perhaps it was left here temporarily by someone else using this path." Sam hurried on, not wanting to miss his ride. That evening as he was returning home, coming down the path in the woods, he saw the suitcase in exactly the same place. "Strange," thought Sam, but he continued on his way home.

The next morning he again found the mysterious suitcase sitting as it had been the day before, next to the large tree. Sam stopped and examined it more closely but could find no name tag on it. He lifted it up, noticing how well it fit in his hand. He also noticed that it wasn't light, and it wasn't heavy but that it felt "just right." Sam thought to himself, "Sure would be nice to own such a beautiful traveling case. You don't find any leather work like this today." He returned the strange suitcase to its place beside the tree and continued on his way to work.

For the next five days, both coming and going, he passed the unclaimed leather suitcase. On the evening of the fifth day Sam took the suitcase home with him. He placed an ad in the "lost and found" column of the newspaper, but no one responded to it. He tacked a note on the side of the tree, listing his name and address, but no one came to claim the beautiful suitcase. He then attempted to open it, hoping that inside there might be some clue to the owner's identity, but he couldn't open the lock. So Sam took the suitcase to several expert locksmiths, but all failed to open it, saying that they had never seen such a strange lock before. If he wanted to see what was inside, they all agreed, he would have to cut it open with a knife. Since the suitcase was so beautifully made, Sam decided against trying to find out what was inside.

He really enjoyed having the suitcase in his home. He loved to look at it and to hold it. He took pleasure in its fine craftsmanship, even if the suitcase had no practical purpose in his life. I know that it may sound strange to say that Sam looked on the suitcase as a friend, but that is exactly how he felt. Soon he found that he could not be separated from it, and so he carried it with him wherever he went. He carried it to work, while grocery shopping, and even took it along on dates.

One morning as he rode to work with his friend, the ever-present suitcase on his lap, his friend summoned the courage to speak to him. "Sam," said the friend, "you know, this suitcase thing was a good laugh at first, but now it's just plain silly. You're a walking joke to the other men at work. You're never going to go anywhere in the company as long as you insist on carrying that suitcase with you wherever you go." As his friend talked, Sam realized the truth of what he was saying. "Yes," thought Sam as they

139

drove along, "it's not logical at all. There's no sense in this attachment. Everywhere I go, people treat me as if I were a simpleton. A suitcase is something appropriate to carry on a trip but not to take to work or on a date!" As they were crossing the bridge over the river, his friend suddenly stopped the car and said, "Sam, get rid of that damn suitcase, now! Throw it out the window and be done with it." Moved by the common sense of his friend's advice, Sam threw the suitcase out the car window. It sailed high over the railing and sank in a silent splash of muddy river water, disappearing from sight. When they arrived at work, Sam — without the suitcase — was greeted warmly by his fellow employees and by the boss. "It sure feels good," thought Sam, "to be back among the old gang again."

That night he stayed out late with some friends, and as he was climbing the steps of his porch he tripped and stumbled. As he stood up to see what he had fallen over, he saw the brown leather suitcase, wet and muddy. He took it inside and with great care cleaned and dried it. That night he slept peacefully, his arms wrapped around his beloved suitcase.

From that time on Sam's life was completely changed. He insisted on carrying the suitcase everywhere he went. Naturally, only those who didn't mind being a companion to an oddball remained his friends. When intelligent people attempted to show him how unreasonable it was to carry a suitcase everywhere, he would only smile and say, "You've never had a suitcase as a friend."

Sam also went only to those places that would allow him to bring along his suitcase. At first there was no real problem in taking it to church — a few strange looks and smiles, but nothing more. One Sunday, however, the pastor stopped him and said in a sharp tone, "This is enough! You're not in a bus station — this is the house of God. Please show the proper respect and do not bring that old, brown bag to church any more." But Sam insisted. The next Sunday when he arrived, suitcase in hand, an usher stopped him and demanded that he leave the suitcase in the entrance foyer. Sam refused, and after a heated discussion he left, never to return. Thereafter, Sam and suitcase prayed together frequently at home, in the woods or while walking down the street.

Quite naturally, Sam's family was worried about his emotional stability. They saw him as a source of embarrassment and would have liked to hide him away. But except for his passion toward the suitcase his behavior was perfectly normal, and so they were unable to find legal grounds to confirm their opinion of his insanity.

As time passed, Sam lost a series of jobs and girl friends. He was a lovable person, except for this thing about the suitcase. One girl did continue to date him, much to her mother's concern. She, however, reminded her mother that a woman shouldn't attempt to change a man before she's engaged, but only afterwards. Sam fell deeply in love with her, and soon they were engaged. One night while on a date, as they were entering a movie theater, some people started joking and laughing about the suitcase Sam was carrying. Losing her patience, his financee' began to cry, saying that she couldn't go on being with him as long as he had that blasted suitcase. Sam was a victim once again of logic and reason and, this time, of tears. He agreed that he would give up his suitcase for her. She was delighted, and before he could change his mind she took the suitcase and threw it atop a passing junk truck on its way to the city dump. That night, on returning to her apartment from the movie, she buried Sam with affection. As they made love on the sofa, Sam became aware of someone else in the darkened

141

apartment. He raised his head and, looking over by the door, saw the brown leather suitcase watching him through the leaves of the large, green philodendron. He said goodnight and goodbye to his girl friend and never again attempted to get rid of the suitcase.

By now he realized that it was no accident that he had found the suitcase in the woods. The suitcase had not been lost; it was Sam who had been lost! Now he had been found, however, and never again would he be parted from the suitcase for any reason or any person. Finally Sam did find a woman who was willing to love him and his suitcase both, and they were happily married for many years.

As you might guess, many strange stories grew up over the years around Sam and his suitcase. The most common was that he was a miser, and not trusting banks he carried with him, at all times, a great fortune hidden inside the old brown bag. Sam far outlived his wife and most of his family. Only a couple of nephews remained alive, and, considering their uncle to be crazy (though they secretly lusted after the "great wealth hidden in his suitcase"), they called him "silly Sam, the suitcase man." On his ninetieth birthday, after a long and happy life, Sam died alone and unattended — but not really alone, since they found him the next day with his arms wrapped around the suitcase and a broad smile spread over his face. Since rigor mortis had developed, it was necessary to take both Sam and the suitcase to the funeral home. After his nephews made the necessary arrangements for his funeral and burial, they rushed home to open the brown leather suitcase. They placed it on the kitchen table, and taking a butcher knife they cut it wide open, like a huge brown watermelon. They stood looking down in amazement at its contents — for the suitcase was completely empty!

142

The Great Diamond

The small jewelry shop was located halfway down a narrow alley that led off from 47th Street. As the customer entered the tiny shop, a small brass bell attached to the door jingled the news that a seeker of treasure had entered. The customer's name was Jason, a well-dressed man in his late thirties or early forties. He carried an oversized brown briefcase in his right hand. The sound of the bell caused the jeweler, who had been seated at a workbench behind the tall counter, to rise slowly to his feet. He had black hair and a black beard, and he wore the small, black skullcap and long, black coat that are customary for Hasidic Jews. To his eyeglasses was attached a single, highly magnified lens, the type used by those who do intricate work. The special magnified lens caused the right eye of the jeweler to appear twenty times the size of his left eye. Jason had the uneasy feeling that the jeweler was looking right inside him, exploring the very corners of his soul.

"I have been told by very reliable sources," said Jason, "that you have here the most perfect diamond in all the world. I would like to buy that precious gem."

"The great diamond," answered the jeweler, "is most rare and therefore very costly. What are you willing to pay for such a marvelous diamond?"

"Everything, if necessary," said Jason. "I have brought a small fortune with me." He opened the briefcase and revealed that it was full of one thousand dollar bills, all wrapped and stacked neatly, along with stacks of bonds, stocks and deeds to various properties. "All this I am willing to give if the diamond is as beautiful as they say."

The jeweler looked at the fortune in the briefcase and said, "Perhaps it will be enough, we shall see." Then he turned and opened a large wall safe, removing an iron strongbox. Opening the box he removed a dark purple velvet bag; and, finally, out of the bag he produced an enormous diamond, as large as a baseball. The great diamond caught the dim light of the tiny jewelry shop and spangled it outward causing the small room to become a whirling carrousel of dancing rainbows.

"It is beautiful — beautiful beyond my imagination," whispered Jason as he stared at the magnificent gem. "I will pay whatever you ask in order to possess it. Please, may I see it more closely?"

"Yes, of course," said the jeweler as a mysterious half-smile came upon his face, "if you wish."

Jason took the diamond from the pale hands of the jeweler with the single great eye and walked over to the window. He held the diamond up to the afternoon light as it streamed through the dusty window. What he saw overwhelmed him, for it was the vision of ten thousand sunsets blended with ten thousand sunrises. As he looked closer at the giant stone, he saw that in the very center was a small circle of pure white light. Looking even closer, he saw that it was a tiny hole, a tunnel that ran through the center of the diamond. He placed his eye to the tunnel and looked through it. His whole being was drawn down its clear, crystal passageway whose sides were intricate, transparent, geometric designs. All time stood still as he made this strange and splendid journey. Slowly he lowered the diamond from his eye and said, "Beautiful beyond words. I will give anything to possess such a diamond."

The jeweler fixed him with a piercing glance and

said, "Such a precious jewel cannot be bought simply with money; you must also give me yourself!"

Jason felt a cold wind suddenly streak through his heart. He had never before in his life given himself to anything or anyone. Success had been his mistress and his lover. His rapid climb to fortune had been unheard of, and now he was being asked to give up something more than his company's ownership, more than all the wealth he had ever acquired. Slowly he answered, "Yes, I will even give myself. I don't know exactly what that means, but you can have that as well." He pushed the briefcase across the counter to the jeweler, and as they shook hands he placed the diamond in his pocket. "Thank you," he said, "this has been a most remarkable day. It's getting late and I must be going home."

"I am sorry," replied the jeweler, "but I did not tell you when you asked to see the diamond that those who look down its mystic passageway can never again go home! Once you have seen inside of things, inside of Life . . . I am sorry, but it is then impossible to return to where you were before. No, my friend, it is not you who possesses the Great Diamond; it is the diamond that possesses you! And I am afraid that there is another reason why you cannot go home. The deed to your home is here inside your briefcase, part of the payment for the diamond. But I am not greedy, and you can't live on the street. Here, I will give you a place to live." He opened a drawer and took out a piece of paper. "This is a deed to an old roominghouse on the south side. You can live there and make a decent income from the rent until you decide to trade in your diamond."

As the jeweler spoke, his single, Cyclops-like eye seemed to burn a hole in Jason's heart as though it were a magnifying glass focusing on a piece of paper in the sun. Then a sharp, piercing pain raced across

145

Jason's head. He brought his hands over his eyes in a gesture that clearly spoke of his discomfort and said, "Excuse me, I seem to have a bit of a headache."

"Fear not, the pain will pass quickly," the jeweler assured him, "but till then you may wish to wear these." He handed Jason a pair of dark sunglasses. "They will help until the energy balances."

Somewhat disoriented, Jason thanked the jeweler, turned and stumbled out of the jewelry shop. He made his way across town with some difficulty but arrived at the run-down roominghouse around sunset. The doorbell was answered by the housekeeper, a large woman named Gretchen. She was a heavy and plain-looking woman. She had been a prisoner of her body since she was an adolescent. With her habitual grouchiness she welcomed Jason into the rooming-house life. But from the hour that he arrived, he changed the lives of all those who lived there. For example, regardless of what the weather was like, Jason would stand at the window, looking out, and would say, "What a beautiful day! Marvelous, absolutely marvelous!" And since he enjoyed smelling, touching and feeling things, those who lived with him also began to take delight in these often forgotten or overlooked pleasures. His laughter and singing filled the once drab house as if the sun itself had come to live there. As the weeks grew into months, Jason fell in love for the first time in his life. He fell in love with Gretchen. To him, she was the most beautiful woman in existence, and he never tired of telling her that. At first she thought of him only as a brother who always needed something done for him. But as time passed, she fell in love with this strange and humorous man who had appeared out of the blue at the front door. She loved Jason especially because he was not chained to conventions or laws. When walking in a park, even if a sign read "Don't Walk on the

146

Grass," he might take her dancing across the green, rolling lawn.

Jason's hands were special. It was as if he had eyes and ears on the tips of his fingers. Whenever he made love to Gretchen, she felt that he could feel what she was thinking, that his touch knew all.

A year after meeting they were married and lived an enchanted life. Even after they were married, he continued to do unconventional things because, as he told Gretchen, "Love makes a man crazy with a special sort of madness." After they had been married for some time, Jason told Gretchen that he wanted to perform an ancient ritual, the marriage of their spirits — a sort of inner nuptial. Jason said that it was not enough to share names or even bodies, that minds and spirits must be welded together as well. Gretchen agreed, and so one night they joined their spirits. "Now," said Jason following the solemn yet joyful ceremony, "divorce is impossible. When people are only married once, then divorce happens all the time. But for the first marriage to be complete, you must marry your spirits, your very souls, together. Without that inner marriage you will always experience divorce. A separation, a divorce will happen each time you are apart because of work or a trip. The reason why there are so many civil divorces is because so few people have enough love for each other to be able to perform the second marriage, the mystic and inner marriage."

One night before they fell asleep, Jason told Gretchen, "I just asked a favor of God, and he told me that it was granted! I asked that if I should die before you do, my spirit would remain with you until it was your time to leave. So, dear, if I should die, don't grieve, because whenever you need me I will be there. You will feel my presence. I promise you that we shall enter paradise together."

Gretchen kissed him on the nose and said, "You crazy man. I never know when you're kidding and when you're not."

Several months later, one Saturday afternoon, Gretchen needed some cheese for a quiche she was baking, and Jason offered to go to the corner delicatessen for her. As he entered the store a robbery was in process. The two teenage thieves had locked the shopkeeper in the back room and now stood, armed with guns, emptying the cash register. One of them pointed his gun at Jason and said, "Dude, you never saw nothing. We don't want any witnesses."

Jason smiled, "Oh, you don't have anything to worry about. I promise you that I will not remember what you look like. Just like those little statues of the three monkeys: speak no evil, hear no evil . . ." and raising his hands to his eyes he said, "and see no . . ." But he never finished his saying because two gunshots blasted the quiet afternoon air. Jason slowly slumped to the floor.

"You fool," shouted one of the thieves, "you killed him. Get his billfold and let's get the hell out-a here."

The other young thief went through Jason's pockets as he said, "I didn't mean to shoot him, but when he raised his hands I thought he was going for a gun or something." Then, pulling out the objects that Jason had with him, the scared thief continued, "Just some loose change and a couple of bucks . . . and this velvet bag. Feels like there's a baseball in it. The cord is tied in some strange knot." And jamming the velvet bag and the money in his coat pocket he followed his accomplice as they ran out the door of the shop and down the street.

When Gretchen heard the shots, she came running toward the store, still wearing her apron. A small crowd had already gathered on the sidewalk outside.

148

Two police cars with revolving red lights were in the street. When she came near the delicatessen, she pushed her way to the doorway where she saw the shopkeeper and the police officers standing over Jason's body. The storekeeper was telling the police, "I don't know why they shot Jason. He couldn't identify them. You know, officer, he was blind!"

Slowly, Gretchen turned and walked away. She crossed the street quickly, wanting to be away from the crowd and their curious glances, wanting even to be away from the polite but clumsy words of sympathy offered by her neighbors. She wanted only to be alone. Slowly she climbed the steps to the porch of the roominghouse, painfully aware of how empty her life would be without Jason. She closed the door behind her and stood in silence, alone, in the darkened, empty hallway. Tears ran gently down her cheeks as she closed her eyes to the pain. Then she felt a pair of hands come from behind her and slip around her waist. They drew her into a warm and intimate embrace. Gretchen didn't turn around to see who it was behind her. She knew that she was all alone in the darkened hallway.

Ernie

Once there was a man named Ernie who lived alone in an ordinary, one-story, white house, located on a typical tree-lined street in a very ordinary town. Brenda, his wife, had disappeared a year ago, leaving behind only a short note. The note, scotch-taped to the bathroom mirror, read as follows: "Dear Ernie, neither of us is happy. I'm leaving. Before I die, I want to experience a little life or adventure and maybe find some love. Brenda."

One month to the day after Brenda's disappearance, the research plant where Ernie had worked for most of his life went out of business overnight. Though he had graduated from college, by education and training Ernie only knew how to do one thing, and now that, like Brenda, was gone.

Ernie found another job, but he did not enjoy it. His life became a procession of losses. So many familiar things changed that any day he expected to hear on the evening news that the Pope had resigned in order to marry a Hungarian princess. His garage was filled with boxes of things that he had purchased but not used since he expected them not to work properly and was prepared to return them. Upon use, most of the things *did* have to be returned — because they *were* faulty.

The paralysis came upon Ernie so gradually that he wasn't aware of it. He failed to notice that many of the things which he had once done so easily were now impossible for him. As a result his life became constricted; his movements limited to going to work, coming home, and repeating that simple pattern. He watched countless hours of television, mostly reruns of old movies. Once a good athlete, now he only watched others at play, and because of the paralysis became a perpetual spectator.

Ernie had also recently come to love antiques; his house was crowded with them. He preferred old things because they had that delightful aroma of another time, and anyway they seemed more beautiful than new things. And the windows of his house, like those of his neighbors — and for that matter, those of everyone in town — were painted over on the inside with delightful, old-fashioned pictures. A grey barn, a quiet, green pasture, images of street scenes of former times and other pictures were either painted or pasted on the windows so that the people could not see outside. What Ernie and his neighbors did not want to see was that their little town was dying: abandoned stores, empty houses and disrepair everywhere. But most of all, they did not want to see the forest.

The forest that surrounded the town had been there ever since the town's beginning. But then it was miles and miles away; it was so distant as to be a source of stories and legends. But within the last few years something strange had begun to happen. The once-distance forest was now approaching the town by leaps and bounds. It now stood closer than anyone wished to acknowledge. The forest loomed on the horizon, dark and foreboding as giant thunderstorms. The tree tops of the forest billowed upward into the sky, ominously dark. Who knew what evil lurked in the forest which daily and with ever greater speed moved in on them?

At first people pretended that the forest wasn't even there or that, if it were, it would never reach the town in their lifetime. Like Ernie, most of the people of the town preferred to watch television as much as possible and to take comfort in the pretty pictures painted on their windows. Ernie agreed with all the other citizens that it was the business of the government to do something because the forest was too large a problem for any of them.

One Saturday afternoon, in the middle of his favorite TV sports program, a knock came at Ernie's front door. He hated to be interrupted while watching TV; it wasn't like a book which you could put down and pick up again without missing anything. And so, with a feeling of resentment, he went to answer the door. When he got there he could find no one. Pleased at this "reprieve," he started back toward his great, brown easy chair and his ball game. But once again there was a knock, and so Ernie turned around and yanked open the door. Once more, no one was there — or so it appeared. Then he glanced down and saw a small child looking up and smiling at him. With the reflexes of a quarterback Ernie closed the door shouting, "I don't buy cookies from kids." But faster than Ernie was the child's foot which shot forward and blocked the door from being completely closed. "Wait a minute," said the child, "I'm not selling cookies or anything else for that matter. I have come to cure you."

"Cure me?" responded Ernie with surprise. "Cure me of what? I'm not sick." Slowly he opened the door, noticing how attractive the blond-haired child was. The child smiled again and said, "I have come to heal you of your paralysis and to bring you the gift of happiness."

Now, as any good doctor will tell you, the most difficult patients to cure are those who do not know they are sick. Ernie didn't feel paralyzed — or at least no more than anyone else he knew. And what did the child mean by "the gift of happiness"?

While Ernie stood at the doorway, lost in

thought, the child had quickly slipped into the house and immediately went to one of the windows. Ernie turned around and saw, with horror, that the child was beginning to peel off the painting of the old covered bridge from one of his windows.

"Stop, stop!" yelled Ernie. "What are you doing?"

"Don't be afraid of the forest," answered the child. "Why must you feel that the unknown is always filled with dread and evil? Why can't the forest be the home of good and beautiful things? The unknown is also the source of exciting surprises!"

Ernie rushed to the window and quickly began to tape up the old-fashioned picture again. As he did he spoke angrily to the child, "Get out of my house. Who can love what they do not know? That's childish immaturity. Leave me alone and let me get back to my ball game."

"I will leave," answered the child, "but I will come back tomorrow with an ancient cure for the poison that prevents you from being happy. I promise you that it will cure you of the impotency of your life." With that the child disappeared. And when Ernie went to the door, he could see no sign of the child anywhere.

The next day, Sunday, when the knock came to his door, Ernie was ready and opened it at once. He stood speechless, however, at what he saw on his front porch. There, looking down at him, was a unicorn!

Not a horse, mind you, but a unicorn. The graceful animal looked at Ernie with its deep blue eyes, its white body glistening in the midday sun. The spiral-twisted horn in the center of its head was white at the base, black in the middle, and had a red tip. Because of the distinctive horn, Ernie recognized the creature as a unicorn at once. He marveled at its graceful and

153

noble bearing; the hind legs were those of an antelope and its tail was that of a lion. He had seen unicorns before only in pictures, that is until *this* Sunday. In the icons of the Middle Ages with which he was familiar, he had seen the unicorn standing beside a Christ-figure or one of the Virgin Mary. Some said the creature was a symbol of purity; others were unsure why the unicorn appeared in the holy pictures. Ernie had also seen them pictured in the royal coats of arms of England. And he remembered that the horn of this fabulous beast was a protection against poison!

"May we come in?" asked a soft voice. Ernie recognized the voice as that of the child, and looking to the farther side of the unicorn he saw his small visitor of the previous day. Speechless, Ernie nodded his head in agreement. And the child and the unicorn entered the house.

"Take off your shirt, Ernie," said the child as the eyes of the unicorn flashed like giant, blue stars. Slowly Ernie removed his shirt. The child came over to Ernie and held his hand as the unicorn lowered his head. The spiral-twisted, red-tipped horn entered the center of Ernie's stomach with the ease of a hypodermic needle. At first pain radiated throughout his entire body, but the child squeezed his hand, and the pain was transformed into great pleasure. Then the unicorn gently removed his horn from Ernie's stomach. The tip of the horn dripped red with Ernie's blood. Once again the creature's blue eyes danced with delight. Ernie placed his finger in the tiny round indentation at the center of his stomach, the only visible sign that remained of the entrance of the unicorn's horn. He looked at the child and asked, "What should I do?"

The child answered, "You must not wait here in hiding for the forest to come to you. Now you must go into the heart of the forest. You must make it

154

your home."

"I am afraid," said Ernie.

"That's not bad," answered the child, "it's only natural. But the unicorn has healed you of the poisonous fear that freezes spirit, heart and limb."

"What shall I take with me into the forest?" asked Ernie.

"I don't know," said the child.

"What shall I do when I get there?" Ernie asked.

"I don't know," replied the child, "but you will think of something. Just trust."

"If I don't like it in the forest can I come home?" came another question — an important one — from Ernie.

"No," said the child. "No, you can never go back home; those who attempt to do so only live in illusion and death."

"Will you and the unicorn go with me?" inquired Ernie.

"Of course!" said the child, nodding at the unicorn. "Why do you think we came to visit you in the first place?"

With that the three of them left Ernie's house. As they walked down the deserted main street toward the unknown, dark forest, past houses with painted windows and closed doors, Ernie felt fearful and apprehensive. But each time he touched the tiny, round indentation in his stomach left by the unicorn's horn, he felt waves of energizing strength streaking through him. Passing the house of a friend who like many others in town was emotionally paralyzed — as Ernie had once been — the door opened a small crack. "Hey, Ernie," came a voice, "where do you think you're going without a shirt on?"

Ernie shouted back, "We're on our way to the forest. We're going to live there. Want to come along with us?"

"No!" returned the neighbor. "Ernie, you must be crazy." And with a quick, frightened glance toward the thick mass of trees on the horizon, Ernie's neighbor slammed the door and returned to watching television with his wife. He said nothing to her, waiting — as was the courteous custom — until a commercial. As the two sterile-looking housewives in the commercial discussed the relative merits of different brands of aspirin, he described the incident to his wife. "Ernie asked me the strangest question," the man related. "He asked, 'do you want to come along with *us*?' I don't understand; he was walking toward the forest . . . all alone."

The Judgement Day

The congenial weatherman, the night before on the evening news, had predicted that it would be a typical spring day — warm and sunny with little possibility of rain. The early morning of this first day of April fit perfectly that weather forecast. However, at about 11:30 that morning an eerie thing happened — a gentle April shower began to fall. What made it so uncanny was not so much the absence of thunder or wind but that not a single cloud could be seen anywhere in the beautiful spring sky! The cloudless April shower lasted no more than twenty minutes, but during that time everyone came out-of-doors to observe this strange wonder of nature.

All the people stood staring skyward as the gentle, warm rain dampened their clothes and their faces. No one seemed to mind the wetness; a few even joked that it must be some cosmic April Fools' Day prank. At about ten minutes before noon the rain stopped, and a giant rainbow arched across the blue eastern sky. Slowly, but quite visibly — in letters of blue, green, red, yellow and purple — the rainbow spelled out a message: "Only those free from the stain of sin shall see God." The cryptic message, while technicolor in its display, was terrifying in its implication.

As people looked to one another for some explanation of this strange phenomenon, their eyes filled with terror; for on each of their faces dark stains slowly began to appear, stains in all colors of the rainbow. Every sin that they had ever committed could be seen on their faces in its own distinctive color. The mysterious rain had caused the once invisible stains to become embarrassingly apparent. It seems that this had been no ordinary April shower; rather, one might say that it had been a doomsday drizzle!

Ashamed that the whole world would now know their personal sins, everyone rushed home hoping to wash away the blemishes. However, no amount of soap or water, of rubbing or scrubbing, would remove the telltale stains of their sins! Peoples' frustration rapidly changed to fear as the thunder began. Low and distant was the rumble, but it soon reached an ear-shattering pitch. From east to west, from north to south, the thunder rolled back and forth across the earth. Once again, everyone hurried outside — but this time it was in panic and dread.

The splendorous rainbow still stood arched across the cloudless sky — but now, in technicolor letters, it spelled out another message: "The world will end in seven days. Only the stainless shall see God." As factory whistles and church bells announced the hour of high noon, a dark shadow slid across a corner of the sun. Within seconds the eclipse was total, and the entire earth was enveloped in a doomsday darkness. It was obvious to all that the eclipse was unnatural and a prophetic forecast of what would happen in seven short days. As the shadow moved away from the face of the sun and the total darkness began to lift, people hoped, for a brief moment, that the return of light might reveal that their stains had disappeared. The return of the sun, however, only disclosed that their faces were still tattooed with the stains of their sins.

No amount of soap, paint remover or cosmetic cream could remove the dye of their deeds, the humiliating revelation of their most secret desires, their hidden thoughts and wishes. Ashamed, people hid in their homes, embarrassed even for members of their own families to see written on their faces every deed and thought of their lives. Strange as it may seem, however, some of the people did not seem to mind the facial doomsday dye. Prostitutes, drunks and thieves roared with laughter as bankers, judges and bishops went about with brown paper bags over their heads as they attempted to hide the immoral deeds of their lives. The embarrassment of the pious church-going folks, whose faces were as colorful as the rainbow, delighted the public sinners.

For the first three days after the mysterious rain shower all were busy attempting to remove their own stains. People tried plastic surgery without success. They prayed as if the world were about to end — which it was — but no amount of prayers could remove the blemishes. Others attempted charity, for was it not true that "charity covers a multitude of sins"? People gave away money to the poor and sold possessions, giving great donations to the Church. After each gift they would run to a mirror, only to discover that their sins still remained written clearly and colorfully on their faces.

Since each deed left its own characteristic color, it didn't take long to determine the code: green for envy and jealousy, red for hate and discrimination, yellow for dishonesty, and so on down the list of human folly. The result was that all the secrets were now public, and each person sat in judgement of everyone else. Marriages broke up, friendships dissolved and so-called heroes and saints were reduced to the level of ordinary folk, of common sinners!

Now the fourth day was Sunday, and everyone — believers and non-believers — crowded into the closest church. The air was polluted with such prayers of petition as "Forgive me, Lord, grant me Your mercy." Long lines — some of them reaching for

159

blocks — formed outside confessionals as everyone sought to be absolved and perhaps — just perhaps — cleansed of the dreadful stains. Sunday morning television had to be cancelled. It seems that the bible-pounding, media evangelists all suffered from a variety of unexpected and sudden sicknesses. Even the Pope did not make his traditional Sunday morning appearance at his balcony; instead Vatican Radio carried only his voice urging all to trust in the mercy of God. As the sun set on the fourth day no amount of church attendance or prayer had diminished the dye of the April shower.

Monday, the fifth day, arrived, and once again the sky was cloudless. Each day at noon the sun began to darken. Each day the length of the eclipse grew, and the dread of the people increased. Since charity, prayer, confession, fasting and good works had failed to remove the stains, people began to fall into depression and despair. No natural catastrophe, plague or war had caused such suffering as did that simple April shower. God had come as a gentle rain. Judgement day had not brought fire or brimstone but rather an apocalyptic April shower!

By the sixth day a sense of frenzy had filled the world; people were vowing complete chastity or poverty, sacred rivers and pilgrimage shrines were jammed with the impure vainly seeking to become pure. People were baptized over and over, as theologians fruitlessly searched sacred scriptures for some last-minute solution. The eclipse on the sixth day extended from noon 'til three o'clock. Weeping and wailing rose from the darkness as many people gave up all hope of being saved and began to consider the possibility of an eternity in hell.

As the world awaited the seventh and final day, some spoke of God's most ancient name in Hebrew, the "Compassionate One." "Surely, the Compas-

160

sionate One will spare us; have faith in the mercy of God," they said. "Because of the stains we can see the deeds and thoughts of each other, but only the Compassionate One can see the intention of those deeds. Only God knows all the facts; even a deed called a sin could have been done out of a good motive. Perhaps such a deed might leave a stain and yet not actually be counted as a sin." Others joined in, "Yes, and some good deeds might be noble in our eyes but could really have been done for selfish reasons; only God sees the intention." But still others reminded them of the rainbow's message: "Only the stainless shall see God." And so ended the sixth day.

With dawn of the seventh day continuous chants began to rise up from the earth: "Holy Mary, Mother of God, pray for us sinners now and at the hour of our death. Kyrie, Kyrie eleison . . . Lord have mercy. Spare your people, O Divine and Compassionate One . . . . "

As crowds of people waited, wailing for mercy, a husband and wife sat visiting quietly. Their marriage had been less than perfect — as is any marriage or friendship. Now, as the end drew near, they talked about the mistakes they had made. Now that their sins, thoughts and even secret desires were plainly visible on their faces, there was no need to be anything but honest.

On the man's face, among other stains, the reddish-purple one of adultery ran downward from the right eye to the chin. He spoke gently to his wife, "You have every reason to despise me, and I would fully understand if you did. But I hope you can realize that you were, and are, the only woman that I have *truly* loved. Can you recognize that, even now at the end, and still care for me?"

His wife's face, especially around her eyes and across her temples, bore the deep green of envy and

161

jealousy. On her cheeks were the dye marks of pettiness and pride. "Yes," she said, "I can, if you can still care for me with all these sins. Yes, I love you still, and it is not at all difficult to say that I forgive you."

Taking her into his arms, he said, "And I forgive you." In the middle of their embrace they found themselves staring in shock at one another, for their sin-stains began rapidly to disappear. Within seconds their faces were not only stainless but radiant with a brilliant beauty. Those in the crowd closest to them spontaneously began to forgive one another. As lightning streaks from the east to the west, so the good news spread across the earth. In the chain reaction, people rushed up to one another — enemies to enemies, one divorced partner to another, parents to children and lovers to lovers — all saying the same thing: "I forgive you." At the end, all humanity wore a face of brilliant beauty.

The hour was high noon, and as the clock struck twelve the whole earth began to heave and to quake as it tumbled out of orbit. Mountains swayed back and forth, sending showers of rocks into the valleys. The oceans, white with foam, churned violently as the sun began to tailspin out of control. At that moment — with an ear-shattering noise — the heavens, like a giant blue egg, cracked wide open. A colossal tidal wave of light — splendorous, intoxicatingly joyful, radiant with energy — came cascading down through the huge crack in the sky — sweeping the earth, and all who lived upon it, out into heavenly space.

<u>the end</u>

On the far outer edges of the circle of white light that had made the wooden table and two chairs a solar universe unto itself, touches of yellow and amber could now be seen. I turned and looked out the front windows of the tattoo shop and could see the first signs of the dawn of a new day. The stories told to me by the Ethiopian tattooist had each one led to the next, until . . . the entire night had passed. How true were his words to me when I entered his shop, "The stories will fill every corner of your consciousness, and there will be no room left in you for pain . . . . " Yes, I thought, and no room for time either.

As the light of a new day rapidly filled the windows I said to him, "Thank you. You were correct. The stories do hold magic. I was unaware that an entire night had passed as you spoke. Your stories took me to far-off lands and also into the dark and strange places within myself."

The Ethiopian showed no signs of fatigue and only smiled and nodded at my comments. Filled with a sense of peace and strength I said to him, "I **would** like to be tattooed. Do you know one more story?"

"No, I am afraid that it is impossible for you to be tattooed. And also, I am afraid that I am out of stories!"

"Why impossible? Is it a matter of time? Should I come back later in the day after you've rested?"

"The reason is," he said, "that there is no room left on you — you are covered with tattoos!"

With an electric shock of alarm I quickly looked at my hands and arms, but they were clean of any sign or mark. I opened my shirt and looked at my chest, but it was also without any tattoo or inscription.

"Be assured that you **are** tattooed, my friend," said the Ethiopian. "Your entire body is covered with

163

the invisible images of the stories which you have just heard, of the parables that I have told you. They are indelibly tattooed on your inner self. They will be a part of you as long as you exist — which is forever. No, my friend, I cannot give you a tattoo because from head to foot you are creatively covered with 22 tattoos."

Contents

 art work of this book is a contemporary interpretation of the art of the Ethiopian Magic Scrolls. As such it is a combination of ancient religious and magical arts and various prayers, united in talismanic symbolism. The prayers that have been interlaced with the art are from Ethiopian Coptic Christian holy books such as *The Net of Solomon, The Apocrypha of Clement, The Life of Adam* and *The Rampart of the Cross*.

The Ethiopian religious art was influenced, it is thought, by the talismanic art of Persia and Islam. Its purpose was to hide as well as reveal, to heal as well as protect, to coax the observer's consciousness to deeper and deeper levels. Unlike much of Western art, its purpose was not to answer the intellect's request for an image to illustrate information or simply to provide an experience of beauty. And so the Book of Exodus (35:31) says of the ancient religious artist, "The Lord has filled him with the spirit of God, in wisdom, in understanding, and in knowledge, and in all manner of workmanship, and to devise curious works . . . to make any manner of cunning work."

Primitive talismanic art has been found in the Ukraine as early as 20,000 B.C., and be it Ethiopian or Celtic, Egyptian or Byzantine, Persian or Chinese, it shows a similarity of style. The interlacing borders, words and symbols, the "curious" knotwork, held a power we do not produce or recognize in contemporary art. In this book the magical knotwork, seals and serpentine forms are freshly interpreted and joined with symbols that hint of the parables that follow in the text.

As the Magical Scrolls and books of the Ethiopian Coptic priests healed, protected and became channels of grace, may the art of this book be talismans for your own journey inward.

BOOKS WERE MAGICAL

for the Ethiopians. Whenever a large number of people could neither read nor write, any book was magic. It held power, ideas and knowledge; yet its treasure was hidden in all those strange, undecipherable symbols which we so casually call letters of the alphabet. Even a book's artwork took on magical powers. Its function was not to illustrate but to cause inner illumination, to cure sickness, drive out evil spirits and to surround the owner of the book in a sorcerer's circle of protection.

Our modern approach to reading is more mechanical than magical. Speed reading or glancing over a page or picture — a "reader's digest" attitude — are expressions of a society without leisure, of a people in a hurry with far too much to do.

168

The art as well as the words of this book are intended to be magical. But if we are to experience this ancient power, we must be willing to sit with story and symbol, allowing them to heal our stunted imaginations and drive out the demons of dullness. If you wish this book to be magic for you, read it slowly and be open to re-reading a parable as often as necessary. While the author may have had his ideas about the meaning of the parable, you may have several of your own! Every true parable holds a cavern of buried insights. Allow, then, the author's reflections after each parable to be a key to open the door of that cavern rather than an intellectual answer which shuts out further exploration.

Parables, as the disciples of Jesus and of other spiritual masters have learned, may not always be immediately understandable. If a particular parable still remains a mystery even after you have read the author's reflection, be free enough to set the parable aside for another time, even another year. Allow the parables the freedom to become teachers, healers or even simply the silent companions of your spiritual quest.

The Magi (p. 13)

All adventures begin with zest and enthusiasm. New roads and idealistic goals attract the curious as well as the courageous. But the comfort of routine, even sacred routine, has an easy attraction that tempts all pilgrims of the Quest to turn back — to make camp with compromises, to lose heart and spirit. The paradox of any Sacred Search is that if we have the perseverence to see it to the end, we realize that we *are* that which we seek.

The Refugees (p. 20)

We are not only what we seek but also Whom we represent. After every social earthquake or religious renewal, the highways and byways are crowded with spiritual refugees. Be we officials or simply observers of this historical reality, we should resist making judgements of others, being devoid of compassion, or promoting laws that only push the refugees even further from the door. Is the Church a private club for the pious or a home for both saint and sinner?

The Cobbler (p. 25)

"Religion" tends to be a secondhand business. But spiritual consciousness, unlike clothing, cannot be a "hand-me-down." To experience the Divine Mystery usually means stepping aside for a time, leaving the business of daily life, climbing the mountain, facing the darkness of the unknown. Without the echo of that experience, rituals of remembering remain tasteless. Worship and sacraments only nourish us if they are in communion with the source of joy, bliss and light. If it is to mend a broken world, the "Message" must be known firsthand.

Smiley (p. 35)

"Religion" thrives on yesterday and technology on tomorrow. The mind loves to ponder the past or play with the future because it finds the present a bore. While the past and the future are necessary places to visit, study and enjoy, they are harmful places to live. To live in the present is to find the fulfillment of the promise of happiness, to see God and live more fully. Stopping the mind, starting the heart and opening the senses should be a frequent inner exercise for travelers on the truly High Way.

The New God (p. 39)

Parables are neither problems in search of solutions nor stories simply to be read — they are symbols to illuminate. And so it is with this parable about time. Time is a measure of our lives like milestones along a highway. To work and live prayerfully in the world is to balance a consciousness of time with an awareness of timelessness. We cannot live without clocks, but we must not let watches watch us or clocks control our lives. Time can be a god, and "being on time," "deadlines" and "timepieces" are his devotions and second-by-second sacraments. When was the last time you enjoyed a Time Out?

The Magic Folger's
Coffee Can (p. 44)

Humanity's blueprints show we were designed to be Blessed. For the "ancient ones," to be Blessed was to be blissful, happy. Daily we feel the hunger for happiness, but often our diets are only junk food. Busy with the business of satisfying that hunger for happiness, we risk starving to death. If you look through the enchanted telescope of the Magic Folger's Coffee Can, you will see that you have at this moment EVERYTHING you need to be completely happy.

The Mountain (p. 49)

Modern life is often machine-like, where home and work are equally mechanical. Life can be Factoryville, and the absence of spontaneity is a warning sign . . . like seeing a dead canary in a deep mine shaft. Death comes slowly on the assembly lines of life, and burial is long after the fact. The assembly line at home or work leaves no room for the "sudden" fancy and the surprise sacraments of life. Fireworks are freakish because they are light — playful, non-productive and eye-delighting. Pentecost made "freaks" out of Factoryvillites.

The Fig Tree (p. 57)

Within the divine plan, we either help God's dream of perfection become a reality, or we abort our part of it. Learning to be "me" means living at peace with the charming, dangerous, saintly, destructive, playful and creative people who live within "me." None of us is one person, a single self, but rather a community of persons. To find oneself is to find the real Self, the divinity dwelling deep within. The Self shines out beautifully when all the various "me's" live in a community of harmony which is pronounced *holiness*. To choose to be "me" is the most redemptive and revolutionary act anyone can perform.

Falling Stars (p. 62)

"Remember you are dust and to dust you shall return" has been the stick-pin of our mortality, but what if we were to see ourselves as "star" dust? Our romance with light is but a form of loving who we

172

really are. Love and kindness cause dead dust and opaque flesh to flash with life. Once again an unpredictable religious renaissance has erupted in a world comfortable with the twilight of devotion and the eclipse of fiery sanctity. Heroes and saints always appear at the bedside of a dying age and the birthing of a new one. To be oneself today, to be "star" dust, can have truly historical and cosmic consequences.

The Soul Dream (p. 68)

God's Will may either be painfully done or joyfully embraced. The Will of God has been the unsolvable riddle of life, used to explain the un-explainable, as the reason to do the un-reasonable. Our struggle to give birth to our dreams even in the face of seeming impossibilities can further the fulfillment of God's Dream. The Divine Dream for the world is not an act of willing but of sharing: God acting with us in concert. Take time to dream. Recall the dream closest to your heart and give it mouth to mouth resuscitation with a kiss of prayer.

The Alien (p. 76)

Religion after the Age of Reason has had the habit of making us aliens, strangers in a strange land. The pre-industrial view was to see the world as home and creation as family. The true function of religion is to make us remember who we are and to make us aware of the rich variety within our family. Those on a spiritual journey, the pilgrimage of Light, do not live in a "no-man's land." They do not journey through a threatening world but rather live, work and pray . . . at home.

The Mirror of God (p. 82)

It is our face, our image, by which we are recognized and by which we know ourselves. The mirror in the story of Snow White had the power to say who was the "fairest of them all." We all long to be the fairest, the most loved. Jesus heard that Voice, "you are my beloved son, upon whom my favor rests," as He saw himself reflected in the mirror of the Jordan. In acts of total self-surrender, in acts of love and service we not only see our "true" image, the Divine Image that is hidden normally from view, but we also hear what we long to hear — that we are truly beloved of God. Each opportunity to die to self for others holds up a mirror magical enough to reveal the "real" us and to speak those words that give the power to give even more! To see oneself in such a mirror is not to lose a part of one's soul as the ancients believed, but rather to find it.

The Board Meeting (p. 88)

Respectability always imprisons. In any age when religion and the arts cease to be valued, they become addicted to positions of respect. Being able to laugh at oneself becomes impossible if we doubt ourselves, living only on the rumor that we are of importance. The revolutionary message in time becomes "tamed" by the keepers of the message; teeth removed, the Word doesn't bite. Words that don't bite easily become pets.

The Banduristy (p. 97)

One of the ironies of life is that imprisonment frequently hides under the guise of freedom and equality. And revolutions often become more rigid than what they refute. In this parable, as in life, surface realities are deceptive; the revolution enslaves, the blind see and the silenced sing. The liberation of the heart lies in the Resurrection. Often in our lives and deeds we become the enemy of the Song, but that does not prevent the resurrection of the Song within us.

The Medicine Man (p. 105)

Nothing in life is free, and that is especially true of freedom. Redemption, grace and life aren't cheap. They require humor, courage and finally the sacrifice of one's very being. But the voice of God is magnetic in its promise of freedom. the world and its custodians — spiritual and secular — locked in their cages of complacency, still find that holy proposition too dangerous. To whom do we listen: those who promise comfort and security or Him whose presence is magic, whose charm is irresistable and who continually pays the price with his own flesh and blood?

The Revolutionary (p. 113)

That the oppressed take on the habits of their oppressors is a law learned in the kindergarten of revolution. Judgement for past crimes and offenses becomes the queen of every revolt, while compassion — justice

175

drunk with love — is never allowed on the streets. Why is God always a friend of the oppressed, even if only yesterday they were the oppressors? As the crowd falls in behind the victors, who walks home with the losers?

Hanna's Harmonica (p. 123)

Keep in mind that this is a parable and not a story. The events, roles and places are to be used as symbols and not taken only at their surface meanings. This parable is about a special kind of insanity. Raw religion, the teachings of Christ if lived out as they were first spoken, would cause us to be "set aside" as either very holy or very insane. Both are beyond the boundaries of "normal" behavior. Jesus himself, we easily forget, was thought insane by his relatives and the other folk of his village. To be considered normal means to make the million compromises necessary to conform — each small, and guaranteed not to "make any difference."

The idea is often repeated in Scripture, "No one shall see the face of God and live!" Before we pray for the gift of the constant Presence of God in our lives, let us seriously consider the consequences.

The Hired Hand (p. 130)

History has shown that religion suffers from travel sickness. The greater the distance and the longer the time from the first Sacred Appearance, the weaker and paler it becomes. Many writers have pondered the question of what would happen if

176

Christ were to reappear among us. This parable looks at that haunting question through another window. Should the disciple who is a mirror of the master be prepared for a case of mistaken identity?

The Suitcase (p. 138)

Words like "pilgrimage," "quest" and "seeker" are classic religious expressions that hold deep meaning, but the reality is that we are sought after by the One whom we seek. We are all called to live as contemplatives, persons whom Love will not leave alone, try as hard as we might to escape. But the contemplative life is for ninety-nine percent of us a suitcase spirituality. The treasure inside is tangible but not visible. Those who are pursued by the Suitcase find that their life partners, their work and their play must, in some way, include the Suitcase.

The Great Diamond (p. 143)

In the Orient they have the expression, "Don't make friends with an elephant trainer unless you have room in your home for an elephant." All discipleship that is true has a cost. Yet the gift of discipleship is to live in the Kingdom where the blind see and death cannot separate. Such a gift is costly, and so the poor in spirit and the cheap of heart should not mail in an order form stamped C.O.D. Let all those with eyes to see . . . see!

Ernie (p. 150)

The plaster is falling on our heads as outside the smokestacks are silent and cold. An age has died and the New Age is daily edging closer. To live between two worlds, two ages, is frightening. Antiques, yesterday's road signs, and the smell of quieter and more secure times are society's pain killers. Yet each day the future comes closer, and we can either embrace it or hide from it. Unless we fantasize, how can the new age be fantastic? The Child and the Unicorn, hope and make-believe, are the vehicles of a second birth. They are also excellent companions for those who have accepted the invitation to accompany the future into the world. Such an adventure as accompanying history — and therefore God — instantly converts fear to love and the quest to a romance.

The Judgement Day (p. 157)

It is impossible for us to act with purity. Try as hard as he might, the most perverted sinner cannot commit a "pure" sin. Nor can the saint perform pure love. Because of Eden's marriage of virtue and fault the most frequent sacrament and common religious experience is that of being forgiven. The failure to forgive, the basic anti-God act, places a tourniquet on the mercy and love of God. Humility and compassion for those whose failings are public are the hallmarks of those who have not denied the invisible stains they bear. They realize that mutual and constant forgiveness is the conditional clause for all divine absolution. To forgive is to give the gift of God; to be forgiven is to be gifted with God.

Dedication

This book is dedicated to some of my teachers in gratitude for the lessons that they attempted to teach me . . . .

Willem Berger
The freedom of the sons of God
Auntie Mame
Life is a banquet
Brian Colombe
The strength of gentleness
Zorba the Greek
The "yesness" of life
Sherlock Holmes
The importance of details
Paul Purcell
Freedom of speech
G. K. Chesterton
The playfulness of paradox
Don Quixote
In the quest lies happiness
Michelangelo Buonarroti
Creativity can increase with age
Norbert Schappler, OSB
Calligraphy
Murray Rogers
The humanity and humor of holiness
Hazel Scott
With honors go responsibilities
Edmund Kestel, OSB
Do what you do with full malice
Swami Abhishiktananda
The real Tibet is in your heart
Gandalf the Grey
Magic and basic wizardry
Patrick Mulvehill
The Celtic cure for aging
Baroness Catherine Dougherty
How to travel lightly

The Author

expresses gratitude to RAY BRADBURY, storyteller and author, whom he met, with empty bucket in hand, at the Cosmic Well . . . .

To DAVID DE RUSSEAU, friend and artist, who patiently critiqued the art work of this middle-aged "folk" artist . . . .

To THOMAS SKORUPA and RUTH SLICKMAN, literary editors, who skillfully decoded the manuscript so that it could be easily read and comprehended. Editing is a hidden art form that requires its own genius and muse. May the editors of this book be blessed for their artful work.

And to his two aunts, MAZIE AND MARGARET HAYS, who taught him, as a small child, a philosophy of life by sharing this poem:

> Through fear of taking risks in life
> I've missed a lot of fun.
> But the only things that I regret
> Are those I have not done.

dward Hays calls himself a folk artist and writer since he has not received any formal training in either art form but enjoys "playing around" with both. He is a Midwesterner, trained by monks of the Benedictine Order at Conception Abbey, Conception, Missouri. His travels in the Orient are reflected in his writing and his present work as priest-director of the contemplative center, Shantivanam, in Easton, Kansas.

Among his hopes and dreams at fifty is that at the end of his life he can echo the words of the Japanese painter, Katsushika Hokusai (1760-1849), who said, looking back over his artistic career, "I have been in love with painting ever since I became conscious of it at the age of six. I drew some pictures I thought fairly good when I was fifty, but really nothing I did before the age of seventy was of any value at all. At seventy-three I have at last caught every aspect of nature — birds, fish, animals, insects, trees, grasses, all. When I am eighty I shall have developed still further, and I will really master the secrets of art at ninety. When I reach a hundred my work will be truly sublime, and my final goal will be attained around the age of one hundred and ten, when every line and dot I draw will be imbued with life." Since the author had a great, great Irish uncle who lived to be one hundred and eleven, he dreams Hokusai's dream.

Credits

While a single name appears on the cover as the author and artist, in reality a small army of artistic and talented people have been involved in the creation of this book:

Managing Editor ....Thomas Turkle

Literary Editor and Layout....... Thomas Skorupa

Associate Editor ....Ruth Slickman

Art Consultant .... David DeRusseau

Editorial Assistant and Promotions...................Jennifer Sullivan

Production Research and Distribution......................Joanne Meyer

Technical Advisor .... Jan Voshart

Literary Advisor ....Stephen Daney

Printing Consultant..................Steven Hall

Production Manager .... Cliff Hall

Typesetter......................Betty Grahnert

Communications....................Eva Curtiss

Paste-up Artist....................Scott D. Beck

Camera Operators.................. Jay Kreipe
Gerald Reed

Negative Preparation.................Ron Emery
Ray Soden

Platemaker ....Denise Thompson

Pressmen......................Michael Taylor
Donald Kennedy

Folding . . . . Patricia Starkey

Bindery Operations . . . . .Greg Lindbloom
Sam McCall, Dennis Peters

Support Staff . . . . . . Ron Allensworth, Neoma Beck,
Barbara Bruner, Randy Bosch, Martin Estrada,
Bud Henderson, Phil Huffman, Susan Kennedy,
Robert Mack, Paulette Stratton, Nancy Wilson

Cover Color Separations . . . . Sun Graphics, Inc.
Parsons, KS

Cover Stock. . . . . 10pt Frankote CIS

Inside Stock . . . . .60# Hammermill Creme

Plastic Cover Coating. . . . . . . McGrew Color Graphics
Kansas City, MO

Forest of Peace Books, Inc.

OTHER BOOKS BY THE AUTHOR:
(available from Forest of Peace Books, Inc.)

Prayers for the Domestic Church
Prayers for the Servants of God
Secular Sanctity
Twelve and One-Half Keys
Pray All Ways
Sundancer